PRIMATE FIELD STUDIES

PRIMATE FIELD STUDIES

Many of us who conduct field studies on wild primates have witnessed a decline in the venues available to publish monographic treatments of our work. As researchers we have few choices other than to publish short technical articles on discrete aspects of our work in professional journals. Also in vogue are popular expositions, often written by non-scientists. To counter this trend, we have begun this series. **Primate Field Studies** is a venue both for publishing the full complement of findings of long-term studies, and for making our work accessible to a wider readership. Interested readers need not wait for atomized parts of long-term studies to be published in widely scattered journals; students need not navigate the technical literature to bring together a body of scholarship better served by being offered as a cohesive whole. We are interested in developing monographs based on single or multi-species studies. If you wish to develop a monograph, we encourage you to contact one of the series editors.

About the Editors:

Robert W. Sussman (Ph.D. Duke University) is currently Professor of Anthropology and Environmental Science at Washington University, St. Louis, Missouri, and past Editor-in-Chief of *American Anthropologist*, the flagship journal of the American Anthropological Association. His research focuses on the ecology, behavior, evolution, and conservation of non-human and human primates, and he has worked in Costa Rica, Guyana, Panama, Madagascar, and Mauritius. He is the author of numerous scientific publications, including *Biological Basis of Human Behavior*, Prentice Hall (1999), *Primate Ecology and Social Structure* (two volumes), Pearson Custom Publishing (2003), and *The Origin and Nature of Sociality*, Aldine de Gruyter (2004).

Natalie Vasey (Ph.D. Washington University) is currently Assistant Professor of Anthropology at Portland State University in Portland, Oregon. Her work explores the behavioral ecology, life history adaptations, and evolution of primates, with a focus on the endangered and recently extinct primates of Madagascar. She has presented her research at international venues and published in leading scientific journals. She is dedicated to educating students and the public-at-large about the lifestyles and conservation status of our closest relatives in the Animal Kingdom.

Apes of the Impenetrable Forest

Apes of the Impenetrable Forest
The Behavioral Ecology of Sympatric Chimpanzees and Gorillas

Craig Stanford

Departments of Anthropology and Biological Sciences
University of Southern California

PEARSON
Prentice
Hall

Upper Saddle River, New Jersey 07458

Library of Congress Cataloging-in-Publication Data

Stanford, Craig B. (Craig Britton)

Apes of the impenetrable forest : the behavioral ecology of sympatric chimpanzees and gorillas / Craig Stanford.
    p.   cm — (Primate field studies)
    Includes bibliographical references and index.
        ISBN-13: 978-0-13-243260-3
        ISBN-10: 0-13-243260-9
    1. Chimpanzees—Behavior—Uganda—Bwindi Impenetrable National Park.   2. Gorilla—Behavior—Uganda—Bwindi Impenetrable National Park.   3. Chimpanzees—Ecology—Uganda—Bwindi Impenetrable National Park.   4. Gorilla—Ecology—Uganda—Bwindi Impenetrable National Park.   5. Competition (Biology)—Uganda—Bwindi Impenetrable National Park.   I. Title.

QL737.P96S723 2008
599.885'15096761—dc22   2006100841

Publisher: Nancy Roberts
Editorial Assistant: Lee Peterson
Full Service Production Liaison: Joanne Hakim
Marketing Director: Brandy Dawson
Senior Marketing Manager: Marissa Feliberty
Manufacturing Buyer: Benjamin Smith
Cover Art Director: Jayne Conte
Cover Design: Kiwi Design
Cover Photos: Craig B. Stanford
Manager, Cover Visual Research & Permissions: Karen Sanatar
Director, Image Resource Center: Melinda Patelli
Manager, Rights and Permissions: Zina Arabia
Manager, Visual Research: Beth Brenzel
Photo Coordinator: Frances Toepfer
Full-Service Project Management: Dennis Troutman/Stratford Publishing Services
Composition: TexTech International
Printer/Binder: RR Donnelley & Sons Company

Credits and acknowledgments borrowed from other sources and reproduced, with permission, in this textbook appear on appropriate page within text.

Pearson Education LTD., London
Pearson Education Singapore, Pte. Ltd
Pearson Education, Canada, Ltd
Pearson Education—Japan
Pearson Education Australia PTY, Limited

Pearson Education North Asia Ltd
Pearson Educación de Mexico, S.A. de C.V.
Pearson Education Malaysia, Pte. Ltd
Pearson Education, Upper Saddle River,
    New Jersey

10 9 8 7 6 5 4 3 2 1
ISBN-13: 978-0-13-243260-3
ISBN-10: 0-13-243260-9

Dedicated to my father, Leland Stanford, Jr.

Contents

What Would Ancient Hominid Coexistence
Have Been Like?

List of Figures

List of Tables

Preface

Having conducted several long-term primate field studies and authored a number of papers and books about their results, I'm delighted to have a chance to tell the story of one such research project in a way that is aimed at college undergraduates. In reading this account of a nine-year research project on the behavior and ecology of chimpanzees and mountain gorillas living in the same African forest, you should think about not only the results, but the way in which a project is planned and put into action. It begins with an idea, proceeds through a set of interesting questions and, if the scientist does his or her job properly, ends up testing hypotheses that may lead to some answers and further research.

Like most scientific studies, the questions build on earlier questions, and are often quite esoteric and narrow. I've tried to set the issues in my study into the larger context of primate behavior. Because my gorilla and chimpanzee study subjects were two of our closest kin, there are also obvious implications for human origins. And although the language of science is often data and statistics, I've tried to keep these clear and concise, to give you a feeling for the depth of the research without overwhelming you with all the details.

For the invitation to write this book, I thank my editor at Pearson/Prentice Hall, Nancy Roberts. I also thank the editors of Prentice Hall's Primate Field Studies series (who happen to be two fine primatologists themselves), Robert Sussman and Natalie Vasey. The editors and an anonymous reviewer provided valuable comments on the manuscript and, as always, I relied on the assistance of friends, colleagues, and some strangers to turn the first draft into a publishable work. For contributions of information, sought-after reference articles, or their advice and perspective on primate behavioral ecology, I thank Drs. John Allen, Maddalena Bearzi, Christopher Boehm, William McGrew, Robert Sussman, Natalie Vasey, and Nayuta Yamashita.

For generously funding the project over nearly a decade, I gratefully acknowledge the support of the Fulbright Foundation (C.I.E.S.), the L.S.B. Leakey Foundation, the National Geographic Society, the Wenner-Gren Foundation for Anthropological Research, Primate Conservation, Inc., and the Jane Goodall Research Center of the University of Southern California.

The nine-year project relied on the good graces of many people. For his initial invitation in 1995 to work in Bwindi Impenetrable National Park, I thank Dr. Eric Edroma, former director of (as it was called at the time) Uganda National Parks. For permission to work in Uganda from 1996 through 2005, I am grateful to the Uganda Wildlife Authority (UWA), the Ugandan National Council for Science and Technology (UNCST), and the Institute of Tropical Forest Conservation (ITFC). In and around Bwindi, I was helped by Drs. Alastair McNeilage, Richard Malenky, Martha Robbins, Nancy Thompson-Handler, Michele Goldsmith, Wardens Christopher Oreyema and Keith Masana, Mr. Simon Jennings, Robert Berygera, Johanna Maughn, Fenni Gongo and his father, Mzee Gongo, Senior Ranger Silva Tumwebaze, Ambrose Ahimbisibwe, and many others. I thank the men of the ITFC staff for their assistance and friendship in the forest and in a variety of permanent and temporary camps over the years. At Camp Kashasha, my project was enabled by the dedicated hard work of Gervase Tumwebaze, Caleb Mgambaneza, and Evarist Mbonigaba, plus a team of local men and women recruited as needed by Gervase. Mitchell Keiver played a key role in the project, and for that and the hardship he endured during the rebel attack in 1999, he has my lifelong gratitude. In the aftermath of that incident, the office of the U.S. Information Service and Mr. Virgil Bodeen were of tremendous help in getting information back to the United States about the situation as it unfolded.

My former graduate student Dr. John Bosco Nkurunungi was the real gorilla side of this project, and he and scholar/conservationists like him hold the future of the great apes of Uganda in their very capable hands. For their help in managing and analyzing the data back at U.S.C., I thank Tatyana White, Laura Verhaeghe, Robert O'Malley, Adriana Hernandez, Xuecong Liu, and Terrelita Price. Finally, for their support of my many trips and absences, I am always grateful to my family: Erin, Gaelen, Marika, and Adam.

Apes of the Impenetrable Forest

1

Introduction

COMING TO THE IMPENETRABLE

August 1995. As the narrow dirt road spiraled up into tortuously steep hills, the little car churned up a cloud of paprika-red dust. We passed tidy villages, children shepherding herds of goats, old men smoking pipes by the roadside. Banana plantations dotted the landscape, their leaves fluttering in the wind like prayer flags. As we went higher and higher, the terraced emerald landscape falling away below us became ever more beautiful. Winston Churchill once referred to Uganda as the Pearl of Africa; if there existed a more stunning scene on the whole continent, I had not yet seen it.

I had come to Uganda from Tanzania on a whim, making the short flight from Dar es Salaam to spend a few days as an ecotourist before heading home to the United States. After several years spent studying wild chimpanzees in Gombe National Park, Tanzania, I had wanted to see my first wild gorillas, and Uganda was *the* place to see them. The travel guidebooks advised me to head to the Impenetrable Forest in the southwestern corner of Uganda, a place now known as Bwindi Impenetrable National Park. I had crossed Uganda by hired car, and had persuaded the driver to continue past the last town up the 60-mile (100 km) dirt track into the national park. We arrived in Buhoma tourist camp at dusk. I paid the driver, booked myself onto a gorilla trek the following morning, and collapsed into the nearest tourist lodge.

The next morning was misty and cool; when I turned up at the trekking departure point a small group of tourists was already assembled. A family of four from California were my main companions for this trek. Each of us had paid $250 for the chance to hike into the mountains of Bwindi to spend one hour with a group of mountain gorillas that had been acclimated to human observers. The guide gave a brief lecture on how to behave in the presence of the gorillas—and what to do if one charged. Then we set off. The forest was alive with birds, but listening was easier than watching; the trails were steep and muddy, coated with wet and slippery vegetation. After an hour of uphill hiking, we broke through the morning mist below us into a blazing blue sky; it seemed like we had walked through the clouds and into the sky.

The gorilla encounter itself was a letdown. The adult male in the group—the silverback—sat in a thicket most of the hour, giving us only occasional glimpses of a broad silver torso. An occasional playful infant or a watchful female made an appearance, but mostly we watched quaking thickets and listened to the rumbling and gurgling of a dozen gorilla stomachs as the apes sat and fed deep in the green undergrowth.

On the hike back to the camp that afternoon, I walked and talked with one of the park rangers who had accompanied us. I told him what I had been doing in Tanzania—a long-term study of the hunting and meat-eating behavior of wild chimpanzees. I began to explain how different my chimpanzees were from these gorillas. But he interrupted me to say that Bwindi had its own population of chimpanzees, too, and he saw them quite often. I was stunned; there were chimpanzees in this forest as well as mountain gorillas? The kernel of a research idea began to grow.

That night in the lodge, I drank beer and swapped Africa stories with the other tourists. Across the bar, a small contingent of African men also sat chatting. I was told one of them was the director of the national park system—the Uganda Wildlife Authority—who was making an official visit to check on the gorilla situation at Bwindi. He was Eric Edroma, a large charismatic man with a booming voice and a back-slapping style. He and I chatted, and when he learned that I was a scientist who studies primates—a *primatologist*—he urged me to come to Bwindi for my next project. I told him what I had learned that morning about the local chimpanzees, and how interesting it would be to learn more about these apes in a habitat they share with gorillas. "Oh, but you must study our gorillas, too," he said. And as I thought about the research possibilities, I saw that he was right—the most interesting thing about the apes of the Impenetrable Forest might be their coexistence, and the possibility that they either competed, or cooperated, or both.

I went back to the United States knowing that my next field project would be about the coexistence of Bwindi apes, a natural follow-on from my previous study of the coexistence of chimpanzees and the animals on which they preyed. It took more than a year and another trip to Uganda to obtain the initial funding for the project from the National Geographic

Society (which would ultimately fund me for the ensuing decade) and to receive research permission from the Ugandan government. I also needed to find a Ugandan counterpart for the project, and to enlist the help of a student or another researcher to undertake research on the gorillas while I focused on the chimpanzees.

By the end of 1996, I was ready to return to Bwindi in earnest. For the next nine years I made regular trips to Uganda to establish a study site, a field research station, and to conduct and supervise the research. The study focused on the ecological relationship between chimpanzees and gorillas. My Ugandan doctoral student John Bosco Nkurunungi became the first African national to do Ph.D. research on mountain gorilla behavior. We learned that our gorillas spent a great deal of time doing things that mountain gorillas were not supposed to do, such as climbing high in trees and eating a fruity diet. Our chimpanzees also did a few things they were not supposed to do, such as standing on two legs to feed on the largest bough in tall trees. We compiled a yearly portrait of the movements of both apes in the area of forest in which our study was located. This portrait was a digitized map of the lives of the two species in coexistence: It revealed patterns of association and avoidance that not only inform us about the biology of the living species, but suggest aspects of the lives of early human species that may have shared a landscape and resources in human prehistory. We obtained at least a preliminary view of the degree to which chimpanzees and gorillas compete, and what happens when circumstances bring them together in the same tree.

BWINDI: THE IMPENETRABLE FOREST

A place with a name as exotic as the Impenetrable Forest ought to have a romantic history. It was the British colonialists who named this densely forested mountain range, but the region—the Kigezi region of western Uganda—was already known as a place of rugged hills and abundant wildlife (Figure 1–1a, b). Although it had been gazetted as the Impenetrable Forest Reserve in 1948, the modern park was created only in the 1980s, when it acquired the name Bwindi Impenetrable National Park. Bwindi means literally "a dark and forbidding place" in the Ruchiga language of the Bachiga people, the culture that is indigenous to southwestern Uganda. The park is 331 square kilometers (Figure 1–2; about 120 sq. mi. latitude 0° 53′ S to 1° 8′ S; longitude 29° 35′ E to 29° 50′ E) and, as the last remaining large tract of montane wet forest in the region, is protected as a UNESCO World Heritage Site. The Virunga Volcanoes, famed as the site of Dian Fossey's mountain gorilla study at Karisoke, sit only 25 miles (40 km) away. But unlike the Virungas, Bwindi is not volcanic and not nearly as high in elevation (1,200–2,600 m instead of 3,000–3,600 m). Its climate is much warmer and, as a result, appears to be far richer in forest trees, especially

(a) (b)

Figure 1–1a, b Bwindi Impenetrable National Park is densely forested and receives abundant rainfall.

fruiting trees. Perhaps as a direct result of this difference in elevation and forest richness, there are no chimpanzees in the Virunga Volcanoes, but a large population of them is found in Bwindi.

Because Bwindi is a mountain range with a great elevational gradient, it is hard to generalize about its climate, flora, and fauna: Conditions in the lower elevations, in the northern region known as Kayonza, are quite different from those in the highest elevations in the southeastern area known as Ruhija (see Figure 1–2). Densities of monkeys are substantially higher at lower elevations, although gorillas are completely absent at the lowest elevations of the park. Whether these differences are due to local flora or climate, or simply because humans in and around the park have had a different impact in different parts of it, is unclear.

Walking through the forest at Bwindi, the terrain and scenery remind me of the Olympic rain forest in Washington State in the United States. It receives roughly 144 centimeters (57 in) of rain a year, although in some years as much as 100 inches may fall (Butynski, 1984). The daytime temperatures at the higher elevations range from 5 degrees Celsius (around 40°F) in the dry, cool winter months of June through August, to about 30 degrees Celsius (about 80°F) during the summer months. There are generally two

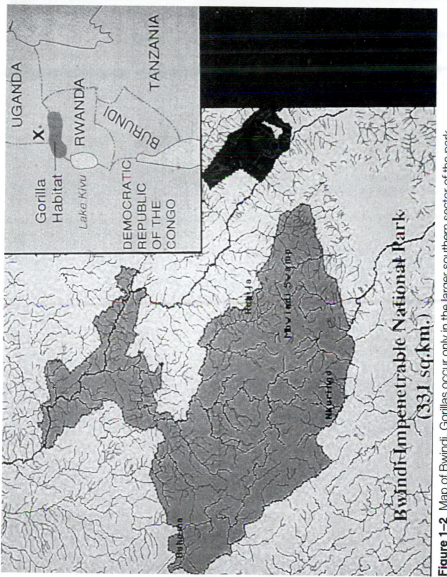

Figure 1–2 Map of Bwindi. Gorillas occur only in the larger southern sector of the park.

seasons of heavy rain, March–April and September–November, although this varies a great deal from year to year.

Lush green undergrowth carpets the ground. There are many clearings, opened by tree falls and maintained by elephant activity; the thick mat of vegetation in these openings is a visual assault of pure green on the eyes. The hills are often so steep that one walks uphill on a nearly vertical slope, grabbing at roots and branches for handholds. Many ravines contain rushing streams. Stands of magnificent tree ferns (*Cyathea*) grow wherever there is soggy soil. Here and there are enormous fig trees, their spreading crowns periodically laden with tiny green fruits that attract primates, birds, bats, and myriad other forest animals.

At the highest reaches of the park, at elevations approaching 2,600 meters (8,500 ft), extensive stands of bamboo (*Arundinaria alpina*) grow. Unlike the Virunga Volcanoes, where bamboo composes the majority of the habitat, in Bwindi it occurs in small and fairly isolated patches, mainly in one very high region of the park. If you hike down the mountain slope in this part of the park, you pass through the bamboo zone—often cloaked in mist—enter an area of tall fruit trees and associated plants, and finally arrive, 600 meters lower in elevation, at Mubwindi Swamp. Mubwindi is one of very few high-elevation swamps in tropical Africa, and is home to a number of species of birds and other animals that occur nowhere else in East or Central Africa. Each evening, as Fraser's eagle owls give their haunting whistles from the edges of the swamp, elephants wade in to feed. Mubwindi Swamp forms the center of the range of both Bwindi gorillas and chimpanzees in that part of the park, as well as foraging habitat for elephants, antelopes, and other large mammals.

The gorillas in Bwindi Impenetrable National Park number approximately 320 as of the latest census done in 2002. Of this number, a small fraction have been habituated for close observation by researchers or tourists. In the Buhoma section of the park, at 4,500 feet (1,490 m) elevation at the western park boundary, several gorilla groups are watched every day of the year by tourists in the company of park rangers, guides, and a few soldiers. A dirt road from the nearest town, Kabale, terminates at the Buhoma park gate. Along this road, just inside and outside the park, are rows of tourist accommodations, from elegant to very basic, along with the many shacks of local people earning a living selling sodas to the tourists, and foodstuffs to the lodges.

Across the hilly parklands, some 20 miles (30 km) to the east as the eagle flies, is the park's research headquarters at Ruhija. The base of operations for the Institute of Tropical Forest Conservation (ITFC), which administers research in Bwindi, sits on a flattened hilltop. In these days of satellite technology, the ITFC headquarters keeps in close touch with the outside world. A decade ago, it was cut off from most communication: now, there are satellite phones and Internet hookups, allowing researchers to read the morning news and sports scores from abroad when not actually camping in the forest. A dirt track stretches along the ridge top near the station, running through the bamboo zone and toward the park gate.

Ruhija is a place of stunning beauty. The incredibly steep trails wind their way from the road to the swamp, passing through dense forest and open glades. Signs of gorilla, chimpanzee, and elephant activity are abundant. Ruhija is a birdwatcher's paradise; there are a greater variety of endemic (occurring nowhere else) forest birds here than in any other mountainous forest in Africa. In a few spots in the forest, primitive campsites have been created, allowing us to pitch our tents to sleep within easy walking distance of the chimpanzees or gorillas when they are ranging far from the research station. Although it is a difficult place to work because of the rugged terrain and frequent rains, the rewards of vistas of the Virunga Volcanoes rising in the distance, and the apes up close, make the forest a wonderful place to do research.

WHY BWINDI?

Bwindi Impenetrable National Park is one of the most beautiful landscapes on the African continent, and also one of the most biologically important. But there are many such forests in a continent as large and geographically diverse as Africa. What brought me to Bwindi was the unique situation of chimpanzee–mountain gorilla coexistence. Gorillas occur across equatorial Africa wherever reasonably undisturbed forest still exists, and in many of these forests (generally those with the least human disturbance), chimpanzees also can be found. But these are nearly all lowland gorillas (*Gorilla gorilla*), and the habitat is almost entirely lowland tropical wet forests. In only two small forest tracts, Bwindi and the nearby Virungas, does the much rarer eastern species of gorilla (*Gorilla beringei*) occur. And as chimpanzees do not occur (may never have occurred, although we cannot be certain) in the Virungas, Bwindi is the only place to examine the relationship between mountain gorillas and chimpanzees in the wild.

Why do we care about how chimpanzees and gorillas coexist? There are two very important reasons, both related to a better understanding of the evolutionary process. First, evolutionary thinkers since Darwin have understood that the presence of competitors in one's environment is a key force molding the evolution of each species. Such competition could be for a variety of resources: food, water, shelter, or simply living space. A fundamental principle of ecology is that of competitive exclusion: when two species of animal share the same space, they must differ in some aspect of their biology, or else one species will inevitably drive the other into extinction, at least in that locality. Of course, similar species coexist in nature, but if you look closely, there are always subtle differences separating even very similar, closely related species. Walk into your backyard and notice the several species of sparrows that visit. To the casual observer they all look pretty much like . . . well, like sparrows, brown and little with thick bills. But conduct a bit of research on them to learn how they actually spend their time and you will find that one species searches for its food on the ground, another only in low tree limbs, and a third only in the tree-tops. One may eat hard-shelled seeds whereas the other specializes on pine cones. And one may breed and nest in April, the other in June. These species differences are not coincidental; they evolved over thousands of years to enable a species to exist in a habitat already occupied by other similar species.

When we see two large-bodied apes sharing the same forest we therefore must ask: How similar are they, and what aspects of their respective biologies are the key points of ecological divergence? The answers to these questions have long existed for chimpanzees and gorillas. The problem is that, as we shall see, these answers have for the most part been wrong. Based on the early field research by pioneers such as Jane Goodall, Toshisada Nishida, and Dian Fossey, we constructed a dichotomy of differences in behavior and ecology between these two African apes (Table 1–1).

The stereotype of gorillas as sedentary meadow grazers—the cattle of the primate order—originated with Dian Fossey's work. Fossey studied gorillas in the high mountain meadows and *Hagenia*-forests of the Virungas, which are the most inhospitable environment in which any ape lives anywhere. The Virungas are cold and wet and almost devoid of fruit or fruit trees. The gorillas there travel very little, pushing their way through meadows full of ferns and thistles and highly fibrous leaves every day, munching as they go. What they consume is highly available, but not very nutritious or calorie-rich. Studies that followed Fossey's showed, however, that we had been misled by the Virungas gorillas to think that most of the species lived that way. As it turns out, as one travels westward from Uganda and Rwanda across the gorillas' equatorial range, the habitats tend to be lower in elevation, far more fruit-rich and tropical, and the gorillas don't behave like Virungas gorillas. Instead, gorillas of the lowlands, from the Democratic Republic of Congo (D.R.C.) to Nigeria, live mainly in lowland rain forest, and eat as much fruit as they can get their hands on. The false image of gorillas as grazers came

Table 1–1 Chimpanzee–Gorilla Ecological Differences: The Conventional Wisdom

Trait	Chimpanzee	Gorilla
Diet	Mainly ripe fruit	Mainly leaves
Travel Patterns	Long-distance travelers	Sedentary, slow
Forest height	Mainly in trees	Mainly on ground
Society	Multimale communities	One-male "harems"

about because the mountainous sites where the earliest studies had been done happened to be marginal, anomalous habitat for gorillas—holding only a few hundred of the tens of thousands of the animals that still live in the region. Had the first studies been conducted in rain forest, our view of these apes, and also of their relationship with chimpanzees, would have been dramatically different.

Gorillas are also often said to be lumbering ground-dwellers, limited to the floor of the forest because of their enormous bulk. Chimpanzees, meanwhile, are agile, powerful climbers. And it certainly is true that chimpanzees are more highly adapted to life in the trees. However, gorillas in many forests forage in the treetops. Chimpanzees may feed in fruit trees, but they travel almost entirely on the ground. Because the Virungas don't have many fruit trees, the gorillas there have little incentive to climb (less than 1% of their diet is fruit; Watts 1984). Bwindi, on the other hand, is fruit-rich (Nkurunungi 2005), probably due to its lower elevation and warmer climate. There are, as a result, trees for climbing everywhere, with tasty fruits as well as flowers and even fungi growing at the top. So gorillas climb when they need to, and chimpanzees spend much of their lives on the ground, contrary to the conventional wisdom.

A third dichotomy is that chimpanzees are highly mobile travelers, walking miles every day in search of their ripe fruit diet, whereas gorillas amble about slowly, covering little distance. This was also based on the observation that at Fossey's Virungas site, the gorillas walked only a few hundred meters a day. But subsequent studies done in other parts of Africa (e.g., Tutin & Fernandez 1985, 1993) showed gorillas walking about as far as chimpanzees do every day. We will examine the reasons for this in the next chapter.

I began my study at Bwindi thinking I knew the differences between chimpanzees and gorillas. As it turned out, the dichotomies outlined in Table 1–1 were largely false, or at least far less stark than I had believed. I expected chimpanzees and gorillas to have points of ecological divergence; therefore, I needed to look for more subtle ways they differed than those offered by the conventional view. And that required long-term study.

At the end of 1996 I returned to Uganda for what became the first of numerous research trips. Some trips lasted several months, some a month or two, and some as little as two weeks. In the beginning, we needed to find the best place in the national park to conduct the study, which meant surveying portions of the park for chimpanzees and gorillas. We also needed to consider logistics: where to live, how to support ourselves day to day, and the personnel required for the project. These "small details" became nearly all-consuming, as they do in most field projects. The chapters that follow present both the scientific results and rationales of the research, and the story of how we set up and ran the project.

2

Great Apes: A Primer

WHY STUDY GREAT APES?

Six million years ago, a creature walked the Earth that was not quite human, but was also different from any ape. This creature was our own direct ancestor, and it also shared a common ancestor with modern chimpanzees. Anthropologists would love to know more about how these creatures lived, because that information might inform us about our own species and where we came from. But apart from a small number of fossils, the physical evidence of our earliest ancestors is still quite limited.

There are, however, ways we can fill in a portrait of our *hominid* (early human) ancestors. This is where primatologists come in. Primatology is the study of our closest kin, the primates. Because we too are primates—one of about 250 species—we refer to our relatives as the nonhuman primates. Of these many species, just four are great apes: the orangutan of Sumatra and Borneo in southeast Asia (now often considered two species, *Pongo abelli* and *P. pygmaeus*); the bonobo (*Pan paniscus*), a close relative of the chimpanzee and found only in central Africa; the chimpanzee; and the lowland and mountain species of the gorilla. Of these, the chimpanzee and gorilla have received the most attention from human evolutionary scientists, perhaps unfairly. Jane Goodall's pioneering study of chimpanzees is now in its fifth decade, and Dian Fossey's work with mountain gorillas is still being carried out today by scientists and their students. They have taught us that they are intrinsically fascinating animals, and also have informed us a great deal about the nature and roots of the human species.

CHIMPANZEES

Of these four apes, we are most familar with the chimpanzee and gorilla because of the legacy of Goodall and Fossey. Goodall's work began in 1960, when famed fossil hunter Louis Leakey sent her to a hunting reserve called Gombe, on the shore of Lake Tanganyika, where he had heard a large population of wild chimpanzees could be found. Leakey had been excavating fossils at Olduvai Gorge, a dry ravine that three million years earlier had been the home of apelike hominids. He saw the natural behavior of wild-living modern apes as a wonderful opportunity to shed some light on how his human fossil behaved in life. This insight, and Goodall's astounding success, formed the basis for the past 45 years of human evolutionary research involving nonhuman primates (Figure 2–1).

Goodall planned a study in Gombe (today called Gombe National Park) that would last several months. It has now reached its fifth decade. She initially gleaned information about Gombe's wild chimpanzees by sitting on a high rocky point overlooking a valley from which she occasionally glimpsed chimpanzees walking past below her. Wanting a closer view of the animals, she cleared a patch of forest and put out bunches of bananas. These were a powerful enough attractant that the shy apes soon lost their fear of her, and the first intensive observations of wild chimpanzees began.

Figure 2–1 Jane Goodall with one of her gombe chimpanzees, Freud. Goodall pioneered the modern science of great ape field studies in 1960.

What Goodall learned about chimpanzees forever changed the way we look at ourselves. She documented their tool manufacture and use—the way they employ twigs and blades of grass to fish termites from their nests. She saw mothers and infants displaying the same close bond that human mothers and their children all over the world share (Goodall 1968, 1986). In the 1970s, a decade after the world had been convinced that chimpanzees and we are cut from the same evolutionary cloth, she reported brutal killings, intercommunity violence, infanticide, and cannibalism. We now realize that chimpanzees, like humans, are an amalgam of nurturing and aggression, scheming intellect and raw emotion.

Chimpanzee society is one of the most complex of any mammal. Chimpanzee field study began in the early 1960s; it wasn't until the mid-1970s that anyone figured out their social organization. Toshisada Nishida began a field study not far from Gombe in 1965. His name is little known in the west, but Nishida became the Japanese counterpart to Goodall, documenting many of the same behaviors—meat-eating, intercommunity killings, tool use—that Goodall had described a few years earlier (Nishida 1990). It was Nishida and his team who realized how chimpanzees live. What seemed at first to be a total lack of grouping—Goodall had surmised chimpanzees to be utterly promiscuous—began to resolve itself. Unlike most other higher primates, chimpanzees do not live in stable, cohesive social groups. Instead, they live in a more fluid system we call a community, made up of anywhere from 25 to 125 individuals. The community has a well-defined territory, defended by the males against neighboring communities. Within the community membership, males tend to be highly sociable with one another, spending much time grooming, hunting, and patrolling their territorial boundaries (Figure 2–2). Male chimpanzees stay in the community of their birth their entire lives, so we might assume that male relationships and alliances are based strongly on kinship—brothers and cousins socializing together—but DNA studies have shown that this is not necessarily the case (Goldberg & Wrangham 1997; Mitani et al. 2000).

Chimpanzee party size and composition can vary widely among study sites. Colin Chapman and his colleagues (1994) reported average monthly party sizes from about one to twelve at Kanyawara in Kibale National Park, Uganda, with a mean size of 5.1. In Taï National Park, party sizes are somewhat larger, ranging from eight to ten (Boesch 1996). At Gombe, Mt. Assirik, and Mahale, mean party sizes are between five and seven individuals (Nishida 1990; Goodall 1986; Tutin et al. 1983). Party size is thought to be influenced by the presence of swollen females (Goodall 1986; Stanford et al. 1994b; Matsumoto-Oda et al. 1998; Newton-Fisher et al. 2001), the size and distribution of fruit patches (Wrangham 1975; Chapman et al. 1994), or some combination of both (Furuichi et al. 2001; Mitani et al. 2002).

Within community ranges, individuals tend to utilize different core areas (Wrangham 1975). The daily and yearly ranges of chimpanzee males

Figure 2–2 Male chimpanzees tend to be highly social with one another.

tend to be larger than those of females (Wrangham et al. 1996). Male chimpanzees are generally more sociable than females, and they seem to prefer the company of other males (Nishida 1979; Goodall 1986). Females spend most of their time with their offspring, rarely joining large foraging parties. Estrous females provide an exception to this pattern, being both highly sociable and strongly attractive to males.

Female chimpanzees, on the other hand, are not very social at all compared to males. They tend to spend their lives alone with their youngest offspring, though the degree of sociality varies from community to community. We believe a female chimpanzee's primary goal in life is to rear her offspring successfully, and anything that interferes with that goal—such as too many other females competing for food with her—is something she avoids. So most females travel individually, becoming social mainly when they are reproductively cycling and actively looking for males. However, during the 9 to 10 days of the 37-day menstrual cycle during which the female bears a sexual swelling, everything changes (Figure 2–3). She gravitates to males, and they gravitate to her. The immediate source of the males' attraction to a fertile female chimpanzee is her swelling. It is a pink, football-sized bag of fluids and tissue that vividly signals to everyone that she is sexually available. Males appear to be highly stimulated by it visually (although some females' swellings evoke a much stronger reaction than others), and given how persistently some males attempt to sniff the genitals of the females, perhaps via odor as well.

Figure 2–3 When ovulating, female chimpanzees possess a fluid-filled sexual swelling that elicits much interest from males.

The sexual swelling of the female did not evolve for the convenience of interested males. Primatologists believe female swellings evoke male interest and male competition to ensure females have the optimum chances to mate with the males they prefer. Female chimpanzees are, as Goodall observed early on, highly promiscuous, sometimes mating with several males in the same hour. Because only one male will fertilize her, it is likely that female chimpanzees secure and maintain bonds with multiple males via mating with them. Moreover, not all sexual swellings a female undergoes involve ovulation. Anovulatory swellings may be more numerous than ovulatory ones over the course of a female's reproductive lifespan. We are not certain why swellings occur independent of ovulation, although no doubt fluctuations in the levels of female hormones induce swellings to inflate and deflate.

The female chimpanzee reproductive system has important conse-quences for chimpanzee life in general. In fact, despite the assertions and assumptions of an earlier generation of mostly male primatologists about the centrality of males, females clearly "drive" the social system in most primates, and indeed most social mammals. We now believe that female social mammals have at the heart of their biology a need to find food resources adequate to nourish and rear offspring. A male, on the other hand, has the ultimate goal of maintaining proximity to the females in hopes of fathering those same offspring. Despite the tendency for males of many mammal species to be larger and more imposing (a trait called sex-ual dimorphism), it is the females' choice of males with those physical traits that have led to their evolution.

In chimpanzee society, females are active seekers of mates, not passive recipients of male mating ambitions. At or after puberty in her early-teen years, a female migrates to a neighboring community, and establishes her-self as a breeding member of that new group. Such females almost always migrate when their swellings are prominently inflated—this is their pass-port, as it were, to be received with open arms by the the new commu-nity's males, who are always eager for new mates.

Males, meanwhile, remain in their natal community throughout life. In addition to the alliances that form through such lifelong associations, males use their intracommunity bonds for two essential purposes. First, they routinely patrol the boundaries of their territories. The males of the community set off toward the periphery of their range, an unmarked but well-known point at which their territory overlaps with that of the neigh-boring chimpanzee community. They are stealthy and silent on reaching the border areas: This is risky business. Should they come upon a chim-panzee from the adjacent community that has strayed into their land, they will likely attack savagely, and often lethally. If the stray neighbor is a young, fertile female, the males may welcome her; males and older females are more often killed or injured (Goodall 1986).

Although such encounters between parties of neighboring communities' chimpanzees have often been called "warfare," they bear few elements of human warfare. Typically, there is an unplanned ambush or run-in between small groups or, more often, one small group and one individual. If a group of several male chimpanzees encounters a group of equal or great size (something it may judge by listening to calls [Wilson et al. 2001]), it will almost invariably beat a hasty retreat rather than engage the enemy. In this, patrolling males are very much like a human military patrol sent out to monitor enemy activity. While their goals include capturing stray enemies, the last thing they are anticipating is a pitched battle with another group of chimpanzees. Richard Wrangham (1999b) has argued that male chimpanzees employ an imbalance-of-power calculation to their territoriality, attacking only when they clearly outnumber the enemy. This sort of arms-race caution explains why actual battles are far rarer than excited encounters with the neighbors that prompt both sides to flee in opposite directions.

These patrols probably serve multiple purposes, one of which is certainly reproductive. Reproductive females are sometimes brought back by the patrolling males to become resident breeding community members. Some chimpanzee communities seem to consist of nearly separate groupings of males and females; in Gombe in Tanzania, each female tends to occupy her own small range, with all the males' travels overlapping hers. At other sites, such as Mahale in Tanzania and Taï in Ivory Coast, females seem to play a more integral and cohesive role in the community.

In addition to reproductive control of females, males also gain access to a great number and variety of fruiting trees by controlling more territory. We have no evidence that health or reproductive success of wild chimpanzees is correlated with the size of their community and concomitant food abundance, but it makes sense that a community would derive nutritional benefits from a larger foraging area. Over the decades of research in Gombe National Park, a clear trend is evident in the size of the territory of the Kasakela chimpanzees (the main study community there) being related to the number of males present in the community in a given year or decade (Goodall 1986).

A second important outgrowth of male bonds in chimpanzee society is hunting. Most species of nonhuman primates eat animal protein, mainly in the form of insects and other invertebrates. Only a few of the higher primates eat other mammals on a frequent basis. In the New World, capuchins of the genus *Cebus* are voracious predators of a variety of smaller animals, including squirrels and immature coatis. Baboons can also be avid hunters of small mammals such as hares and antelope fawns, and in at least one site, meat-eating by baboons was as frequent as for any nonhuman primate population recorded. Only in one great ape, however, do we see the sort of systematic predatory behavior that we believe began to be a part of our early hominid ancestors' behavior between two and three million years ago. Chimpanzees occur across equatorial Africa, and in all forests in which they have been studied intensively, they prey on a variety of vertebrates, including other mammals (Figure 2–4). At least 35 species of vertebrate prey have been recorded in the diet of wild chimpanzees, some of which can weigh as much as 20 kilogram. One prey species, the red colobus monkey, is the most frequently eaten prey in all forests in which chimpanzees and the colobus occur together. In some years, chimpanzees in Gombe National Park, Tanzania, kill more than 800 kilogram of prey biomass, most of it in the form of red colobus.

Figure 2–4 A Gombe chimpanzee with its red colobus monkey prey. Chimpanzees are systematic predators on a variety of other mammals.

We know a great deal about chimpanzee predatory patterns (Stanford 1995, 1998). At Gombe, red colobus account for more than 80% of the prey items eaten. But Gombe chimpanzees do not select at random the colobus they will kill; infant and juvenile colobus are caught in greater proportion than their availability (75% of all colobus killed are immature; Stanford et al. 1994a). Chimpanzees are largely fruit eaters, and meat accounts for only about 3% of the time they spent eating overall, less than in nearly all human societies. Hunting is primarily a male behavior (nearly 100% of all kills in most study sites are made by males). Adult and adolescent males do most of the hunting, making about 90% of the kills recorded at Gombe over the past decade. Females also hunt occasionally, though *more often* they receive a share of meat from the male who either captured the meat or stole it from the captor. Although lone chimpanzees, both male and female, sometimes hunt by themselves, most hunts are social. In other species of hunting animals, cooperation among hunters is positively correlated with greater success rates, thus promoting the evolution of cooperative behavior. In both Gombe and the Taï forest, Ivory Coast (Boesch & Boesch 1989), there is a strong positive correlation between the number of hunters and the odds of a successful hunt.

The amount of meat eaten, even though it composed a small percentage of the chimpanzee diet, is substantial. I estimated that in some years, the

45 chimpanzees of the Kasakela community at Gombe kill and consume hundreds of kilogram of prey biomass of all species (Stanford 1998). This is far more than most previous estimates of the weight of live animals eaten by chimpanzees. During the peak dry season months, the estimated per capita meat intake is about 65 grams of meat per day for each adult chimpanzee. This approaches the meat intake by the members of some human foraging societies in the lean months of the year. Chimpanzee dietary strategies may thus approximate those of human hunter-gatherers to a greater degree than previously imagined.

In the early years of her research, Jane Goodall noted that the Gombe chimpanzees often went on "hunting crazes," during which they would hunt almost daily and kill large numbers of monkeys and other prey. The most intense hunting binge we have seen occurred in the dry season of 1990. From late June through early September, a period of 68 days, the chimpanzees were observed to kill 71 colobus monkeys in 47 hunts. It is important to note that this is the observed total, and the actual total of kills that includes hunts at which no human observer was present may be one-third greater.

Hunting by wild chimpanzees appears to have both a nutritional and a social basis. In his pioneering study of Gombe chimpanzee predatory behavior in the 1960s, Teleki (1973) considered hunting to have a strong social basis. Some early researchers had said that hunting by chimpanzees might be a form of social display, in which a male chimpanzee tries to show his prowess to other members of the community. Wrangham (1975) conducted the first systematic study of chimpanzee behavioral ecology at Gombe and concluded that predation by chimpanzees was nutritionally based, but that some aspects of the behavior were not well explained by nutritional needs alone. Nishida (1990) and his colleagues in the Mahale Mountains chimpanzee research project reported that the alpha there, Ntologi, used captured meat as a political tool to withhold from rivals and dole out to allies. McGrew (1992) has shown that those female Gombe chimpanzees who receive generous shares of meat after a kill have more surviving offspring, suggesting a reproductive benefit tied to meat-eating.

Some of the most important and widely publicized results of chimpanzee field study have been about tool manufacture and use (Figure 2–5). Chimpanzees have shown themselves to be the most technologically skilled creatures on Earth after human beings. Chimpanzee tool use varies widely across Africa, although the mosaic pattern of occurrence suggests that appearances and extinctions of local tool technologies may occur frequently. Certainly there is no evidence that the occurrence of particular tools is related to either ecological or genetic differences among chimpanzee populations (McGrew 1992). Instead, chimpanzee tool-use patterns appear to reflect local cultural traditions that arise in individuals and spread within, and perhaps among, breeding populations.

Figure 2–5 A chimpanzee using a blade of grass as a termite fishing probe.

Some tool-use generalizations can be made. Three broad categories of tools are found: stick tools that are used to increase either arm reach or lever arm strength; sponges, made of chewed leaves to absorb fluids; and hammers, made of wood or stone and used to crack open hard-shell food objects. In eastern Africa, stick-tools are used to fish for termites and ants, to probe honey, food and, occasionally, to brandish against intracommunity rivals. These traditions themselves vary among nearby communities. In Gombe National Park in western Tanzania, chimpanzee fish for termites from earthen mounds using simple twigs stripped of leaves (Goodall 1986).

In Mahale National Park, only 100 kilometers away, chimpanzees fish for ants from tree trunks using the same methods (Nishida 1990), but never apply this tool to termites in mounds, although they are abundantly available. In Taï National Park in Ivory Coast, western Africa, chimpanzees use stones or wooden clubs to break open nuts and hard-shelled fruits (Boesch & Boesch 1990). In Gombe, despite an abundance of rocks of suitable size and widespread nuts and fruits of species related to those in Ivory Coast, chimpanzees have never been reported to use stones as hammers.

Cultural variation in general is widespread in chimpanzees. In the wild, chimpanzees display regional variation mainly in behaviors such as tool-use practices and grooming styles. A few symbolic behaviors vary cross-culturally as well, such as leaf-clipping (clipping leaves with the front teeth to indicate frustration [Bossou, Guinea], or sexual interest [Mahale, Tanzania], depending on the local culture). Chimpanzee display by far the most varied and widespread degree of cultural variation. Whiten et al. (1999) presented a systematic analysis of tools and other cultural aspects of chimpanzee societies in seven long-term study sites across Africa. They distinguished among anecdotal, habitual, and customary use of such tools, and showed that in at least 39 cases, cultural behaviors including tool use show a pattern of customary use, more reasonably attributed to learned traditions than to ecological influences on the pattern.

Goodall's study at Gombe continues today, although new technologies and new ideas have led to research questions unthinkable in Goodall's early days. DNA paternity testing confirms parentage (Constable et al. 2001), urine testing confirms the hormonal basis for male and female sexual behavior (Muller & Wrangham 2004), and video cameras allow in-depth analysis of behaviors long after the events have transpired (Muller et al. 1995). Five other study sites have seen twenty or more years of field research (Table 2–1), with even more studies of a decade or more. And still, as investigations into the lives of our closest relatives approach the half-century mark, our ignorance about chimpanzees still outweighs our understanding of them.

Table 2–1 Long-Term Chimpanzee Field Studies

Site	Location	Year	Primary Researchers
Gombe	Tanzania	1960–	Goodall, many others
Mahale	Tanzania	1965–	Nishida, many others
Budongo	Uganda	1962–64, 1991–	Reynolds, Plumptre
Ngogo	Uganda	1982–84, 1995–	Mitani, Watts, Ghiglieri
Taï	Ivory Coast	1979–	Boesch and Boesch-Achermann
Kanyawara	Uganda	1987–	Wrangham

GORILLAS

The largest of the world's primates—males can weigh up to 450 pounds in the wild—gorillas have always occupied a place of honor in the human psyche (Figure 2–6a, b). Since the earliest reports of savage giant apes in the heart of Africa, westerners have tried to penetrate their veil of mystery. After a few early twentieth-century expeditions that photographed and filmed the giant apes in the wild, wildlife biologist George Schaller conducted the first field study (1963), and showed that gorillas are anything but savage. The first long-term study of gorillas was done by Dian Fossey, who immersed herself in the lives of several groups of mountain gorillas living in the Virunga Volcanoes of Rwanda for more than a decade. She described the animals living in small harems, with one silverback male— his torso graying over as he reached sexual maturity—at the center of each group. Fossey's mountain gorillas were the source of all our understanding about this species for many years. As more field studies were done, scientists realized that "her" mountain gorillas represented but one variation on a theme for these apes, and that other populations living in other parts of Africa were quite different, both anatomically and behaviorally.

Until the 1990s, we classified all gorillas in Africa as the same species (*Gorilla gorilla*), but the rise of genetic work and continued field studies

(a)   (b)

Figure 2–6a, b The gorilla is the world's largest primate: silverback males (a) can weigh up to 200 kilograms (440 Pounds). Younger males (b) are called blackbacks.

Table 2–2 Long-Term Gorilla Field Studies

Site	Location	Year	Primary Researchers
Karisoke	Rwanda	1969	Fossey, many others
Lopé	Gabon	1983–2004	Tutin
Kahuzi-Biega	D.R. Congo	1978–79, 1987–	Yamagiwa
Mbeli-Bai	Rep. Congo	1993–	Olejniczak
Mondika	Rep. Congo	1994	Doran-Sheehy
Nouabale-Ndoki	Rep. Congo	1989–	Kuroda
Bwindi	Uganda	1984	Butynski, J. B. Nkurunungi, M. Robbins

have led to a reclassification (Table 2–2). Today, most authorities place western and eastern gorillas in two separate species (*G. gorilla* and *G. beringei*, respectively). Moreover, a tiny remnant population of gorillas in eastern Nigeria, the so-called Cross River gorillas, are often considered a separate subspecies, *G.g. diehli*. Eastern gorillas are also divided into two subspecies, or races: the eastern lowland gorilla (*G. beringei graueri*) and the mountain gorilla (*G.b. beringei*). It is this last mountain subspecies that comprises the gorillas of both Bwindi and the Virungas. Although a few primatologists have argued that Bwindi and Virungas gorillas should themselves be split into two taxa (Sarmiento et al. 1996), the weight of genetic (Garner & Ryder 1996), anatomical, and ecological (Stanford 2001) evidence warrants considering them the same population, divided into two only with the last several hundred years by human-caused deforestation (Hamilton et al. 1986).

The irony of the "how many species and subspecies" issue with respect to gorillas is that populations that look very much alike may be separated by millions of years of evolutionary time. In western Africa, western lowland gorillas are found in numerous patches, large and small, of remaining tropical forest. These lowland gorillas share the same basic body size, skeletal anatomy, and the short grayish hair with chestnut cap that characterize all western gorillas. However, these similarities belie that fact that some outwardly identical populations have been disjunct from one another almost as long as chimpanzees and humans have been on separate evolutionary lineages (Gagneux et al. 1996). Mountain gorillas in both Bwindi and the Virungas share shaggy jet-black hair, with a saddle of silver developing in males as they mature.

Fossey reported the basic pattern of gorilla social behavior: small, highly cohesive social groups, and an entirely herbivorous diet. (Gorillas disdain the meat that chimpanzees relish, and their insect-eating is limited to occasional pickings made by fingers, not tools.) Fossey (1983) and her students (e.g., Harcourt 1978) showed that contrary to the popular image of the

Figure 2–7 Unlike chimpanzees, female gorillas live in cohesive social groups along with one or more silverback males.

macho silverback controlling a coterie of submissive females, female gorillas are active mating strategists, prone to emigrate from the group in which they live to pair up with other males (Figure 2–7). The result is that most gorilla groups include one or more silverbacks plus a number of unrelated females and their offspring. These females do not for the most part bond strongly with one another, but rather with the silverback (Sicotte 2001)—hence the tendency for groups to fragment when the silverback dies or is ousted. The macho male that appears to be intimidating rival males in other groups may in fact be more worried about his own female bolting from his group to join the rival. Females also leave their natal group after the death of their silverback, in which case all the females may scatter. Watts (1989) and others have documented that such male-less females often lose any dependent offspring they may have at the time to other males. Infanticide is in fact one of the leading sources of mortality for young mountain gorillas, although it apparently does not occur among eastern lowland gorillas (Yamagiwa 2001).

Female mountain gorillas do have social affiliations with one another, albeit at a lower level than is seen in most primate species in which related females form the core of the group (Watts 2001).

A maturing male gorilla faces a choice: stay in the group of his birth and hope the silverback (who may be his father) will share his females (or perhaps be unwary enough that the females can be mated with secretively), or leave the group. Such "blackback" males who leave often spend months or years wandering alone, ultimately attempting to pull females away from other groups to create the nucleus of their own new group. Whether leaving or staying is a more effective strategy at enhancing a maturing male's reproductive success has only recently been examined (Bradley et al. 2005).

Just as the traditional harem notion gave way to newer field data on the nuances of female and male roles in gorilla society, the animals' ecology has undergone dramatic revision since Fossey's pioneering days. Fossey's Virungas gorillas, living in high mountain meadows nearly devoid of the fruit trees that blanket the lowland tropical forests of Africa, eat virtually no fruit. Instead, they eke out a living browsing on the abundant, albeit nutritionally poor, greenery that carpets their habitat. Plowing slowly through thickets of greenery, they have often been likened to cows—living a slow life on a poor diet. Ecologists refer to the undergrowth in a forest as terrestrial herbaceous vegetation (THV) and Virungas gorillas essentially live on it. Another picture emerged, however, once gorilla field research was undertaken in other sorts of forests elsewhere across Africa. Caroline Tutin was the first to show that western lowland gorillas do not live on a leafy diet, nor do they exhibit the same sedentary lethargy of the montane populations.

Gorillas occur across a wide range of habitat types, and their ecology varies accordingly. Most of the information available on gorilla ecology has come from the Parc d'Volcans in the Virunga Mountains of Rwanda. There, mountain gorillas feed primarily on perennially available foliage and other nonseasonal foods (Vedder 1984). Mountain gorillas select foliage that is high in protein and low in tannins and fiber (Watts 1991); not all plants within the home range are eaten, nor are they always eaten in direct proportion to their availability (Fossey & Harcourt 1977).

By contrast, western lowland gorillas eat a diet rich in fruit. In Equatorial Guinea, 40% of their diet was composed of fruit (Jones & Sabater Pi 1971). In Cameroon, evidence of fruit was found in 50% of all fecal samples (Calvert 1985). More intensive studies in Gabon (Tutin & Fernandez 1985, 1993; Rogers et al. 1988; Williamson et al. 1990), the Central African Republic (Remis 1997; Goldsmith 1999), and the Republic of Congo (Nishihara 1995) indicate a highly frugivorous diet. Although large amounts of fruit are consumed, the importance of herbaceous vegetation, as well as other woody vegetation (pith and bark) in lowland gorilla diet should not be underestimated. During certain times of the year, more than 90% of the fecal samples contain fiber and leaf fragments (Williamson et al. 1990).

Gorilla ranging is strongly influenced by habitat and food availability. The day range of Karisoke gorillas is short, averaging 570 meters per day (Watts 1991). Watts found that the effect of group size on time spent feeding was small, which suggests that the costs of social foraging are low for mountain gorillas. Lowland gorillas travel much farther per day; Tutin (1996) found an overall mean day range in Lopé of 1.1 km/day, whereas

Remis (1997) found a mean at Bai Hokou, Central African Republic, of 2.3 km/day. Travel length has been shown to correlate positively with fruit availability (Remis 1997; Goldsmith 1999). At Bai Hokou, there was a significant positive relationship between group size and daily path length during all seasons, suggesting high levels of within-group feeding competition. This result was not found at Lopé (Tutin & Fernandez 1993). In addition, Bai Hokou groups were found to form temporary subgroups that fed and slept separately from one another, perhaps as a way of reducing feeding competition (Remis 1997). Mountain gorilla group size does not seem to influence day range either; in this case due to the widespread, abundant foliage on which they feed (Watts 1991).

The most extensive studies of eastern lowland gorilla behavioral ecology have been done in Kahuzi-Biega National Park. Work in the Kahuzi region (Casimir & Butenandt 1973; Goodall 1977) suggests that the gorillas spent most of the year in secondary forests and migrated seasonally into bamboo forest, where young bamboo shoots constituted approximately 90% of their diet. Large silverbacks often fed on the ground while other individuals foraged in trees, especially when they were in mixed secondary forests (Goodall 1977). Goodall (1977) and Casimir (1975) concluded that the distribution of food was more important in determining the movement of gorillas than the presence of other groups. Casimir and Butenandt (1973) found that gorillas traveled only about 0.6–1.1 km/day.

Until the work at Bwindi was begun, no gorilla population had been examined that exhibited a combination of traits of mountain and lowland gorillas. As we shall see, the Bwindi gorillas share many ecological traits with lowland populations, while being genetically indistinguishable from the other, Virungas, montane population. Bwindi gorillas have shorter hair than Virungas gorillas, but whether that is a locally evolved adaptation or simply due to the colder climate in which Virungas gorillas live (in the same way that your cat grows thicker fur during the winter) is unknown.

THE OTHER APES

Two great apes—the chimpanzee and gorilla—are the subjects of this book. But there are four great ape species in the world today, and the other two bear a mention. One is a close kin of the chimpanzee, and lives in central Africa. The other is the only Asian great ape, and its behavior has long been an enigma.

Bonobos

In the forests of central Africa lives a great ape that clearly shares a strong resemblance, and a recent common ancestry, with chimpanzees. Bonobos

(*Pan paniscus*) were only identified as a species separate from chimpanzees when Belgian hunters and naturalists brought carcasses and skeletons back from the Congo in the 1920s. The original skull, collected in 1927, sits amid the largest collection of bonobo skeletons in the natural history museum at Tervuren in Brussels. From the neck up, bonobos superficially resemble chimpanzees; males are much more robust than females, with much larger canine teeth. From the neck down, bonobo males and females are almost identical, and more slender than a typical chimpanzee.

Bonobos are far less well-studied than chimpanzees, because they live in inaccessible regions of a politically troubled nation, the Democratic Republic of Congo (D.R.C.). The D.R.C. has undergone so many violent political upheavals that long-term research has been frequently interrupted. Unlike the ecologically versatile chimpanzees, nearly all bonobo populations that have been studied live in lowland rain forest, a habitat far more difficult to observe naturalistic behavior than the lower canopy, more open forests in which chimpanzees are often found.

Randall Susman and a team of students began the first modern field study of bonobos in the 1980s at Lomako (Table 2–3). Richard Malenky, Nancy Thompson-Handler, and Frances White documented the basic pattern of social behavior in this species, which is a variation on a chimpanzee theme (Susman 1984, and papers therein). Bonobos live in fission-fusion communities, with females migrating between territorial groups of males. Unlike chimpanzees, male bonobos have not been reported to launch lethal attacks into other communities, although much chasing and lower level aggression occurs. Females from one community have even been observed to mate with males from neighboring communities during such encounters, a most unchimpanzee-like behavior.

Within communities, bonobos show some striking contrasts from chimpanzees. Females bond closely with other females, alliances that they use effectively to thwart aggression from males (Furuichi 1989). One mode of female bonding is genital-genital rubbing, in which females rapidly rub their sexual swellings. This behavior occurs most often when females are confronted with stressful social situations, such as competition for food. Two females attempting to forage in the same tree for the same fruit will rub swellings, which seems to reduce tension between them. It occurs more frequently among juvenile bonobos than among adults, and occurs

Table 2–3 Long-Term Bonobo Field Studies

Site	Location	Year	Primary Researchers
Lomako	D.R. Congo	1975	F. White, G. Hohmann, B. Fruth
Wamba	D.R. Congo	1974–	T. Kano, T. Furuichi
Lui Kotal	D.R. Congo	2001–	G. Hohmann, B. Fruth

more frequently in captivity when a bonobo group is placed together, declining in frequency over time (Sannen, personal communication).

Bonobos travel in temporary subgroups—parties—as chimpanzees do. These parties tend to be larger than those seen in chimpanzees, perhaps related to the bonobos' tendency to feed on more foliage (in addition to ripe fruit) than chimpanzees. Because of their larger party sizes and the extended duration of swelling in females, virtually every bonobo party ever seen at Wamba, for example, contained at least one female with a sexual swelling (Kano 1992). This contributes to the observer's impression that these apes mate more frequently and openly than chimpanzees, but this impression has not been borne out by studies of the mating frequency of both species (Hasegawa & Hiraiwa-Hasegawa 1983).

From recent field research on bonobos, we know that bonobos eat meat less frequently than chimpanzees do, but perhaps more often than we had believed (Hohmann & Fruth 1993). Bonobos are not the accomplished tool makers and users that chimpanzees are. Although there have been reports of bonobos walking upright in a nearly human posture (de Waal & Lanting 1997), there is no empirical evidence that their degree of bipedal walking and standing differs significantly from that of chimpanzees (Videan & McGrew 2001).

Bonobos have deservedly received a great deal of attention from both scientists and the public as one of our two closest relatives. But despite the differences in social behavior from chimpanzees, bonobos are quite similar to chimpanzees in most respects. They and chimpanzees are best seen as two variations on a theme; they are examples of the genetic, anatomical, and behavioral changes that may occur when two populations of the same species become separated (in this case, by the enormous width of the Congo River) for long periods of time, with ensuing evolutionary divergence.

Orangutans

The least understood of the great apes has long been the orangutan (*Pongo pygmaeus*). Although modern field studies of this red southeast Asian ape were begun more than thirty years ago (Rijksen 1978; Galdikas 1985), the largely solitary nature of the species, combined with the difficulty of working in the rain forest, have hindered a full understanding of their socioecology. In contrast to the growing number of sites at which chimpanzees and gorillas have been studied in Africa, only a handful of long-term field studies have been conducted in Asia on orangutans (Table 2–4).

Orangutans live on two large islands in the island nation of Indonesia, Sumatra and Borneo, which is only a tiny relic of their geographic distribution in ancient times (Delgado & van Schaik 2000). These two populations are sometimes considered to represent separate species, *P. pygmaeus* (Borneo) and *P. abelii* (Sumatra) instead of two subspecies. Research on the differences

Table 2–4 Long-Term Orangutan Field Studies

Site	Location	Year	Primary Researchers
Tanjung Putting	Borneo	1971–	B. Galdikas
Gunung Palung	Borneo	1985–	M. Leighton, C. Knott
Ketambe	Sumatra	1971–	H. Rijksen, C. van Schaik
Suaq Balimbing	Sumatra	1993–1999	C. van Schaik

in the ecology and behavior of the two island populations has opened our eyes to the likely causes of sociality and solitariness in the species.

Orangutans are the most sexually dimorphic of all apes; males approach twice the size of females, and possess secondary sexual traits such as widely flanged cheek pads, long hair, and throat sacs for emitting loud calls. An adult male orangutan will occupy a large territory in the forest, attempting to ward off all other sexually mature males. Individual females, meanwhile, occupy much smaller territories with their dependent off-spring. The reproductive goal of each male orangutan is to monopolize as many females as he can. Male orangutans are so big and slow-moving, however, that this is rarely possible. There are numerous other males in the forest who lack females of their own. For these transients, another mating strategy exists. After years of puzzlement over the apparent extended ado-lescence of some male orangutans—some males lack cheek pads and long hair into their 20s and 30s—researchers realized that some male orang-utans do not develop these characteristics. They produce sperm, copulate with females, and likely conceive offspring, all in a preserved state of adolescence (Maggioncaldo et al. 2002). This bimaturism—two modes of males—is unknown in any other primate.

The reason males try so hard to monopolize, or at least have access to, females is that female orangutans have extraordinarily slow reproductive rates. A female matures at about the same age as other great apes, in the early teen years. But her interval between births is extremely long—up to nine years—so her ability to produce babies between about age fifteen and death in her thirties or forties is severely constrained. This interbirth interval make females choosy about their mates, and males eager to capi-talize on any mating opportunity.

Orangutans are largely arboreal fruit eaters. Tool use is seen in some populations, but on the whole this is not a very technologically adept species. But their large bodies require large caloric input, and also a high degree of food selectivity (Leighton 1993). The forests in which orang-utans live are subject to unpredictable, severe fluctuations in food supply, called mast fruiting. Females in particular must be able to survive periods of poor food resources by subsisting on fallback, less desirable foods until high-quality fruits and other foods are available (Knott 1998).

After years studying orangutans in lowland forests in Sumatra, we now know that orangutan sociality itself is a function of food availability. In both Borneo and northern Sumatra, orangutans are found in forests ranging from lowland river valleys to freshwater and peat swamps. They also occur in mountainous forests and in drier forests. But population density shows a strong correlation with the availability of soft pulpy fruit (Delgado & van Schaik 2000). In Borneo, where low-productivity forest predominates, orangutans typically live at very low population densities (1–2 individuals/km²). In Sumatra, in more fruit-rich environments, densities tend to be much higher (5–7 individuals/km²). In general, they live at higher density in peat and swamp forest, as found in Sumatra, and at very low densities in mountains, drier forests, and in dipterocarp forests, which are more common orangutan habitats on Borneo.

The highest density population of orangutans found anywhere may tell us a great deal about the profound effects of food on socializing. Field research by Carel van Schaik and his colleagues (Djojosudharmo & van Schaik 1992; van Schaik et al. 1995) at Suaq Balimbing in northwestern Sumatra, orangutans live at densities some five times higher than in most Bornean forests. Moreover, Suaq orangs are often social, coming together at fruit trees. What allows them to be so social is apparently their food supply, which mitigates the need for spacing themselves and competing aggressively.

Orangutans remain enigmatic to us, with more field research urgently needed. Their conservation status is also perhaps the most critical of the great apes, due to rapid forestation of the small forest patches they occupy.

APES IN COEXISTENCE

Because the orangutan lives only in southeast Asia, and the bonobo lives in forests in central Africa not shared by chimpanzees or gorillas, the only case of sympatry among great apes is chimpanzees coexisting with gorillas. The earliest field studies of gorillas—by Schaller and Fossey—were of Virungas gorillas, which do not live sympatrically with chimpanzees. And the early studies of chimpanzees were all of populations that did not occur in the range of gorillas. George Schaller (1963), in the course of his landmark study of mountain gorillas, reported that local village elders in the Virungas area told him chimpanzees had at one time also occurred there, but were now extinct. In the first study of sympatry, Jones and Sabater Pi (1971) observed the relationship between the two apes where they occurred together, in Rio Muni (now Equatorial Guinea) in west Africa. The researchers spent 17 months in Rio Muni, Equatorial Guinea, observing chimpanzee and gorilla populations, some of which were sympatric. They reported home ranges averaging 5.5 to 6.75 km² for gorillas, and 15 km² for chimpanzees. Feeding and ranging data were limited, but several means of ecological separation were suggested that may have reduced feeding competition between the two species. During wet seasons, gorillas ranged in fairly open areas of regenerating vegetation, while chimpanzees utilized the upper strata of primary equatorial forests. During dry seasons, gorillas were found in dense vegetation at the edge of forests and in primary equatorial forests adjacent to areas of regenerating vegetation. Chimpanzees occurred mainly in the lower strata and on the ground in mature equatorial forests. The gorillas in Jones's and Sabater-Pi's study fed almost completely terrestrially, whereas chimpanzees were mostly arboreal feeders.

In the 1970s, Caroline Tutin, studying western lowland gorillas at Lopé, Gabon, obtained more detailed information about the local chimpanzees, although they were shy enough that in-depth observation was not possible (Tutin & Fernandez 1985). Gorillas at Lopé utilize many of the same foods as chimpanzees; their diet is much closer to that of chimpanzees than it is to that of gorillas living in the Virungas (Rogers et al. 1988; Tutin & Fernandez 1993). The gorillas utilize a minimum of 134 species of plant foods, including fruits from 95 species (Williamson et al. 1990). It appears that they satisfy a substantial part of their energy needs from fruit, relying on leaves to provide protein (Rogers et al. 1990). Fruits that are low in fat content appear to be preferred (Rogers et al. 1990). Most gorilla plant foods (69%) are harvested arboreally (Tutin & Fernandez 1993). Lopé chimpanzees include 174 food items in their diet (Tutin & Fernandez 1993). They are primarily frugivores, utilizing 111 species of fruit (Tutin & Fernandez 1993). Approximately 76% of chimpanzee plant foods are harvested arboreally (Tutin & Fernandez 1993). There is great overlap in the diets of chimpanzees and gorillas at Lopé; approximately 60–80% of foods were eaten by both species (Williamson et al. 1990; Tutin & Fernandez 1993). Gorillas are more likely to feed on THV than chimpanzees are, and are more willing than chimpanzees to concentrate on THV when fruit is scarce (during the three-month dry season). Chimpanzee and gorilla diets diverge most at times when fruit is not abundant; the gorillas shift foraging strategies whereas chimpanzees continue to forage extensively for ripe fruit even in periods of low fruit availability (Williamson et al. 1990). Direct interspecific competition has not been observed.

Research on sympatric gorillas and chimpanzees in the Nouabalé-Ndoki forest of the Congo and Central African Republic has revealed similar patterns of resource use. In Nouabalé-Ndoki, gorillas are more highly frugivorous than any other documented population (Kuroda et al. 1992; Nishihara 1995). Their diet consists of over 63% fruit, which is consumed seasonally. Dietary overlap with chimpanzees is therefore greater, though the data are preliminary (Kuroda et al. 1996). Ndoki gorillas make extensive year-round use of swamp forest (Nishihara 1995) and feed in fig trees in proximity to chimpanzees during times of fruit scarcity (Suzuki & Nishihara 1992).

Eastern lowland gorillas *(Gorilla g. graueri)* and chimpanzees are sympatric in Kahuzi-Biega National Park in eastern Democratic Republic of Congo, and have been studied by Yamagiwa et al. (1994, 1996). Gorillas occur at a density of 0.45 individuals/km^2 whereas chimpanzees occur at a lower density of 0.13/km^2. The higher gorilla density may be related to the chimpanzee frugivorous diet in an area of low fruit diversity. Yamagiwa et al. (1996) found that Kahuzi gorillas eat a more diverse diet (129 food types from 79 plant species) than chimpanzees do (99 food types from 75 plant species). Both gorillas and chimpanzees eat fruit over the entire annual cycle, though not necessarily the same species at the same time. The two apes co-feed on at least four important fruit species, and sometimes feed together in the same tree crown. Gorillas at lower elevations in Kahuzi-Biega eat more fruit than those at higher elevations, apparently related to fruit availability differences (Yamagiwa et al. 1994). Ecologically, this population appears to be intermediate between western lowland and mountain gorilla populations in the degree of frugivory and the plant species diversity in the diet.

This was the background available when the study of chimpanzees and gorillas began in the mid-1990s. We knew that chimpanzees did not occur in the nearby Virungas, so we could compare the possible effects of sympatry with chimpanzees on gorillas in Bwindi, while at the same time comparing the effects of habitat differences. We knew that in the previous studies of both apes in coexistence, one species or the other (usually gorillas) was the main focus of the study, with information on the sympatric species gathered slowly and often incidentally. Yamagiwa's study in Kahuzi-Biega was the most valuable comparison, since his project had detailed information on both gorillas and chimpanzees, and was located only a few hundred km from Bwindi, also in a mountainous region.

We had many questions to ask, and research avenues to explore. But first we had major obstacles to surmount: learning as much as we could about the local apes to pick a study site, establishing a base of operations in a remote forest, and trying to continue the project year after year, with all the logistical, financial, and practical problems that beset any field study. How we began this effort is the subject of the next chapter.

3

Getting Started

There are few more difficult tasks for any researcher than establishing a field research site. You might think it would be straightforward: go out to a remote forest and start walking, and when you find the animals you are there to study, just start watching them and taking notes. But the act of observation, so central to primate behavioral research, is a vanishingly small part of most field studies' early stages. Before you reach that point, there are a thousand things to accomplish and problems to work through. There are three distinct levels to setting up: getting the funds to undertake the study; getting permission from the national and local governments that administer the area where the study is to be done; and, of course, the logistical problems of doing the study itself. That so much valuable primate research has been done over the past four decades is testimony to the dogged persistence of many scientists.

THE IDEA

First comes the idea. It is mandatory in the field of animal behavior that one says the theory behind the work—studying ecological principles—comes first and the choice of the species to study comes second. If you write a grant application that says you want to study chimpanzees because they're so fascinating, you're not going to receive any funds. If, on the other hand, you write that you want to study the evolution of the human diet, and chimpanzees may tell us something important about that, you may well be rewarded with a grant. But it is an unwritten truth that field scientists usually choose the animals they study because they find them fascinating and beautiful. The best armchair thinkers are often helpless in a hot, muggy rainforest; the folks who gravitate toward a career of living in remote areas without electricity or running water tend to want that lifestyle, and also to love watching animals.

Developing the idea and theoretical basis for a field research project comes about through an enormous amount of reading, listening to conference papers, and talking to colleagues. As one begins to comprehend the scope of what has been studied already and what important questions remain, ideas begin to take form. These ideas become research questions, and these questions lead to hypotheses. The hypothesis is the educated guess (based on a great deal of background reading and thinking) about an explanation for the phenomenon that you now plan to study.

For example, in my study, the initial idea was "wouldn't it be interesting to study chimpanzees and mountain gorillas living in the same forest?" It popped up during my first tourist visit to Bwindi in 1995, as I described earlier. The questions quickly followed: "Would they compete for food? How about nesting sites ? And do they ever actually feed in the same tree?" These questions led to hypotheses that predicted expected outcomes. Formulating hypotheses is critically important for two reasons. First, it is the core of your project; hypotheses are explicit statements of the structure of your logic and the importance of your study. It is also vitally important to demonstrate that your project is worthy of funding to the reviewers who will ultimately decide its fate. Many wonderful research proposals have failed because the hypotheses to be tested have not been carefully developed at the outset. You must work at the cutting edge, asking questions and proposing answers that have not yet been answered by others. But if you try to answer a question that is unanswerable—beyond the cutting edge, as it were—you will fail also. So, framing the hypothesis is a delicate balance between the unknown and the unknowable.

SHOW ME THE MONEY

The hypotheses, in addition to being the formal intellectual basis for the field study, are the basis on which one obtains the all-important funding to get started. When you read about a wonderful and exotic field project, whether on great apes or giant pandas, it is easy to forget how difficult it can be to line up sufficient financial backing for the project. Even the most preliminary field study often involves flying to another part of the world, and although costs are often low in developing countries, it takes several thousand dollars for a student to get started in the field. To begin a major project and then keep it going year after year generally requires, at the minimum, tens of thousands of dollars per year. This money can be requested from a U.S. government agency, such the National Science Foundation. Such agencies, however, usually require applicants to be fairly far along in their research—so far along, some researchers complain, that innovative research can be stymied unless the answers to the questions are known before the funds are requested. For the early stages of even the most important and exciting new project, funding is always in critically short supply.

Fortunately, there are a few farsighted private foundations that support research in the field of great ape behavior and human evolution. The National Geographic Society is well known for its magazine and television documentaries, but their research wing has enabled many projects through the years, including those pioneering studies of Jane Goodall and Dian Fossey. The L. S. B. Leakey Foundation, named in honor of the famed fossil hunter, is dedicated to the study of human origins, which includes research into nonhuman primate behavior. The Wenner Gren Foundation for Anthropological Research is another important source of support. None of these organizations typically funds an entire field project, instead giving grants in the neighborhood of $5,000 to $25,000. But they are willing to take small risks on projects with uncertain end results (Leakey in particular funds research by students as well as senior scientists). These three granting foundations are the lifeblood of field primatologists, especially in the early days of a study when the results and success of the project are uncertain. They are often supplemented by grants from conservation organizations, if the species involved are endangered or threatened.

GETTING THERE AND BEING THERE

Generally the first step in undertaking a new field study is to conduct some brief pilot project. This is enormously helpful to get a sense of the feasibility of a longer project, to lay groundwork with local officials who must grant permission for a longer project, and especially to establish some preliminary evidence that indicates to a funding organization that longer study will be grant-worthy. The pilot project is usually only two or three months' duration, and requires funding small enough that one's university or a small foundation grant can cover the costs. You hope to find enough information about your topic to make a longer project intellectually warranted. Of course, in practice, you spend your three months at a new field site wandering around the forest just trying to spot some sign of the still-unhabituated, shy animals you hope to return later to observe in depth.

If the pilot study goes well, the next major step is to return to start the long-term study in earnest. It typically takes a year just to write and submit grant proposals and wait for the funding to be approved, and meanwhile to apply to the local government for a research permit and visa. If the funding comes, you put the rest of your life—house, apartment, family, friends—on hold and head for the field.

But before actually getting into the field one must usually spend days or weeks in the capital city, navigating an often Byzantine labyrinth of bureaucracies to obtain the research permit. Getting the permits can be easy, or it can be a nightmare. It is a common experience to wait hours or days for the right government official to arrive at his or her office, only to be told that you *really* must see a different government official who is out of town until the following week. I try to tell myself during such escapades that a foreign researcher arriving in Washington, D.C., would have a similarly frustrating time getting all the necessary permits to do research in our own national parks. Formal written permission and permit fees are normally required from the government office that administers the forest in which you will work, and then a visa or residency permit from the national immigration office. In a formally protected area like a national park, there may also be an independent research office that co-ordinates and facilitates research, providing logistical help and charging a usage fee. The annual cost for the permits alone can vary widely, from a few hundred dollars to many thousands of dollars, again depending on the country.

You can often avoid all these hassles by studying wild primates that are already being studied by others, so the subjects are accustomed to being followed, and many of the logistical barriers have been negotiated. But that would limit primate field research to just a few sites; the majority of researchers eagerly go after research topics and species that represent the cutting edge. This often means conducting the first study of a little-known species or population. Partnerships with local scientists in the host country can also help to negotiate smoothly the bureaucratic and linguistic barriers to setting up a new project.

Depending on the country, you may have to hold all meetings with officials in a language that is not your own. Field biology is one of the few sciences in which the scientist often needs a working understanding of a second language. This may require enrolling in a French or Kiswahili or Mandarin class, but learning the local language is a must if you are going to employ and rely on local field assistants or students, as most good projects do. And all the while you are preparing to leave, you are still writing grant proposals, trying to sublet your apartment, and asking your significant other to put his or her life on hold for you.

INTO THE WOODS

Once the permits have been granted, you are off. Arriving in the proposed field site after many months of anticipation is exhilarating, and daunting.

If you are working in an area where local people are familiar with the concept of foreigners living in their neighborhood to study animals, you may find a welcoming committee of men and women of all ages who want to apply for the position of field assistant, camp keeper, cook, and anyone else you might need. At the same time, it's important to reach out to local people—if there are any—to ensure they regard you as a friend and not an interloper. In some areas, local people associate foreigners arriving from wealthy countries with having their land appropriated to create wildlife sanctuaries or to reduce human pressure on existing wildlife reserves.

In my own case, the early trips and setup of the project were filled with excitement, and also frustration. It took about a year following the 1995 trip to Bwindi to obtain grant money and research permits to begin the project. But the first question was where to begin? Bwindi is 120 square miles of dense forest. Although the gorilla population was fairly well censused in the mid-1990s, nothing was known about the chimpanzee population. I wanted to locate a place in which gorilla and chimpanzee densities were both high, and where both species could be habituated to our presence so we could observe them closely. That required some exploration, and also some local advice. I learned through e-mail correspondence during 1995 and 1996 that the Uganda Wildlife Authority (UWA; in 1995 it was still called Uganda National Parks) was planning to start a new tourism project within Bwindi. This would open access to a second set of "tourist" gorillas in Nkuringo Valley, about 12 kilometer (8 m) southeast of the ecotourism center at Buhoma (Figure 3–1). It was not an easily reached place; a rough road ran the circumference of the park, passing along the ridge high above the site. But the road ended before reaching Buhoma, which meant that it was useless as a means to reach Nkuringo unless you spent many hours circumnavigating the park in the opposite direction. Although there were plans afoot to extend the road to link Buhoma and Nkuringo, for the time being accessing the new site required a half-day hike across hilly forest and farmland.

Nkuringo had much to offer as a potential field site. First, in anticipation of future tourism and the revenue it would bring, UWA had begun a gorilla habituation program. A rough campsite had been made on a hilltop overlooking the forest, and a contingent of park rangers was living and working there. Moreover, progress had been rapid; apparently the silverback male in the Nkuringo group was a particularly laid-back gorilla who quickly adapted to the daily presence of the humans. After only a few months of fearful flight, the Nkuringo group began to settle down and allow themselves to be observed at close range. In time this group became as approachable as any Bwindi gorilla group and Michele Goldsmith, an early participant in the project, undertook her postdoctoral work on aspects of their ecology.

Figure 3–1 The field camp was constructed on 3 hectares of land in Nkuringo Valley.

The chimpanzees of Nkuringo, meanwhile, were an unknown apart from the frequent sound of their distant pant hoots echoing across the hillsides. During 1996 and 1997, I spent several months a year in Bwindi hiking the hills in search of them. Although we encountered chimpanzees daily, and sometimes spent hours near them, they always kept themselves out of direct view, and fled if we tried to approach too closely. It was only with the help of one of the expert field assistants we borrowed from the Institute of Tropical Forest Conservation (ITFC), Caleb Mgamboneza, that we made progress. Caleb was the star of the team of gorilla research assistants, a tracker extraordinaire who could follow the trail of a gorilla, antelope, or human in terrain where you or I would see no signs at all. He owed this ability to his upbringing as a member of the Batwa. The Batwa are one of the many so-called pygmy ethnic groups in equatorial Africa. Caleb's father had been a revered woodsman, and Caleb had learned much from him. Sadly, the Batwa today are in much the same state of indigenous peoples everywhere: shunted into settlements, treated badly by the larger population, and cut off from many of the traditional forest-based ways of their people. Caleb spoke both the Twa language and Ruchiga, plus some Kiswahili (in which he and I conversed). He also spoke the language of the forest, and could call antelopes from the forest by mimicking their fawns' distress calls. He could identify which direction a chimpanzee had been traveling, and for how long, by the subtle presence of broken twigs and droppings.

Caleb and I camped at the ranger campsite near the mouth of Nkuringo Valley at various times during 1997, trying to establish the size and movements of the Nkuringo chimpanzees. Each morning we would set out into the park to look for chimpanzee nests, chimpanzee droppings (for evidence of food eaten), and above all, the chimpanzees themselves. With lengthy encounters (albeit brief high-quality observations) of the chimpanzees, we began to assemble a profile of the Nkuringo community.

The Nkuringo ranger camp was adjacent to the forest, and its location at the opening of the valley enabled me to learn something about chimpanzees that I had always wondered about. Many researchers have speculated about what chimpanzees do at night. Each adult or adolescent chimpanzees builds its own nest every night. Of course they sleep in their nests, but do they sometimes communicate with one another, or leave their nests to socialize, fight, or feed? In most study sites, the camp where researchers live is a good distance from where the chimpanzees live. In Gombe, where I had lived and studied chimpanzee hunting behavior in the early and mid-1990s, the chimps often nested near the camp, but the location of researcher housing on the beach meant no forests were audible due to the lapping of small waves. Here in Nkuringo I could sit on the hillside in the evening and hear chimpanzee pant hoots—the breathy build-up UH-UH-UH, followed by the wailing hoot—echo off the valley walls. These would elicit more pant hoots from other chimps across the valley. Presumably these animals were lying in their nests, calling out to one another to signal their location. And interspersed among these pant hoots it was often possible to hear the staccato pops of a gorilla chest-beating in the forest. One night as I lay awake in my tent, unable to sleep at 2 A.M., I spent an hour keeping track of the number and frequency of pant hoots, and then did the same the next morning. The rate of pant-hooting was actually higher in the middle of the night, presumably coming from nesting chimpanzees, than it was during daylight hours.

During this period I also began to explore the possibility of adding a Ugandan counterpart to the project. I placed an advertisement at Makerere University, the premier university in the country, for a biologically trained field research assistant. The idea was that a Ugandan could manage the logistics of running a field project in the wilds of his own country, speaking the local languages, and could in return obtain a Ph.D. with funding and supervision from western scientists. Most important, after decades of white North American and European students watching mountain gorillas, there would finally be a gorilla-ologist who hailed from the nation where the gorillas live.

Of the people we interviewed, one stood out. John Bosco Nkurunungi was from Kanungu, in the region of Bwindi. He was completing a master's degree on the parasites harbored by the Bwindi gorillas, and was eager to continue his fieldwork. We agreed that he would become a field research assistant, and I would look for funds that would allow him to enroll for his Ph.D. The data he collected as my assistant would then provide him with the material for his doctoral dissertation. It was also decided that Bosco should begin his work in Ruhija, the high-elevation part of the park where the research headquarters is located, instead of Nkuringo. This would allow Bosco to work on a known gorilla group, the Kyagurilo (often called the research group), and would also contribute to the ongoing habituation of that group for other researchers. Ruhija was already set up with all-weather buildings, a small library, and an herbarium, while at the time we were living in small tents in Nkuringo. At the time, this seemed like a disappointing trade-off; it meant we would study both chimpanzees and gorillas, but in two areas of the park that were at least twenty miles apart. As it turned out, however, the decision to have Bosco working in Ruhija could not have been more fortuitous.

THE CAMP

The project now needed a field staff: a field assistant who could be in charge to run the data collection in the absence of any supervisor, and someone to run the camp. Although Caleb was an ape tracker without equal, his reading and writing abilities were limited, and he did not write at all in English. But as soon as I made it known that we were in the market for a local person to work as the head field assistant, I was approached by Silva, a senior park ranger. Silva was one of those people who has genuine leadership skills, and to whom others look for guidance. He was from an influential local family that owned a large piece of land bordering the park. Silva told us he had a younger brother, Gervase (then age 25) who would be interested (Figure 3–2).

Gervase quickly assumed the mantle of field coordinator for the project. He had a high school education and spoke and wrote English fluently, but most of all he had the work ethic that any field researcher dreams about finding in an assistant. Although he did not know the forest or its inhabitants well initially—he had spent his life as a farmer—he took to his work in a highly motivated way. Caleb quickly became his tutor in all things Bwindi-related, and in time Gervase became the most skilled and knowledgeable of all the local field assistants in matters relating to chimpanzees, their habitat, and their diets.

At about this time, we also made it known locally that we would be needing a cook/camp keeper; someone to take care of researchers so they could spend their entire day in the forest and not have to worry about preparing meals. Not long afterward, as I hiked into the Nkuringo land from Buhoma, a young man was standing on the trail awaiting my approach. He greeted me with outstretched hand, smiling confidently and telling me he

Figure 3–2 The field assistant team, left to right: Mitchell Keiver, Gervase Tumwe-baze, and Caleb Mgamboneza.

was the camp keeper I was seeking. Evarist turned out to be all that and more. In time, he mastered cooking—and made delicacies for dinner that were rarities for me in primitive conditions.

Before I had spent much time in the field with Gervase, I needed him to help with a more immediate task, the construction of a more permanent camp than the tented campsite in which we had been working. This would allow us to live as close to the forest as possible and would provide housing for the field assistants who would run the project in my absence. By agreement with UWA, we planned to construct the camp using only local traditional materials—wood beams, doors, and windows. Mud was to be used as the wall stucco, along with palm thatch roofs and dirt floors. This was so the camp would quickly return to a natural state should we terminate the project.

First, we needed a plot of land on which to build. Gervase fortuitously had three uncles, one of them a senior park ranger as well, who jointly owned a plot of land south of the ranger camp. The family was wealthy by local standards, and their considerable land was planted with bananas, sorghum (used as cattle fodder), and corn. Because of the mountainous terrain, the hillsides were terraced, and every usable spot of land was cultivated. But the land nearest the park boundary was not very useful to them—the gorillas, chimpanzees, baboons, and bush pigs periodically made forays from the forest into the crop fields, destroying entire fields of banana plants in one night. So the land nearest the park was left fallow. Desidereus, the ranger uncle who did much of the negotiating, offered me a plot of about six acres of his farmland that ran down to the Kashasha River (really a narrow rushing stream).

With the newly employed Bosco (Figure 3–3) leading the negotiating for us, we spent a rainy afternoon pacing off the boundaries of the land being offered us. The land was so steep that the lower portion was not visible from the upper portion, even though the distance was only a couple of hundred meters. Most of it was overgrown brush on long-abandoned cropland. There was a natural clearing of sorts in the center, where we planned to build the camp. Cold, clean drinking water poured from a natural spring in the mountainside on one side of the land. In front of the plot, all views were of the dark green forest looming above. It was a visually stunning location, and in a part of Bwindi that was little known biologically.

As we paced off the land boundaries, using a panga (similar to a machete) to cut a swath of trail that would demarcate our new property, we came across a fat rhinoceros viper, a preternaturally beautiful—and also deadly—snake with a skin mosaic of green, brown, and purple, and a two-pronged appendage on its snout that gave the creature its name. The

Figure 3–3 John Bosco Nkurunungi collecting data for his doctoral thesis on gorilla diet and travel patterns.

group of locals who accompanied our outing wanted to see it killed. I took its presence as a good omen (this species turned out to be alarmingly abundant in and around the forest) and asked that it simply be placed back in the brush, on our side of the new boundary markers. All in all, it seemed a propitious start.

I refer to this transaction, in which funds from the Leakey Foundation and the University of Southern California acquired the camp land, as a purchase. But because of complicated national laws in Uganda restricting foreign ownership of land, it was really a long-term lease signed between the newly named Bwindi Impenetrable Great Ape Project (BIGAPE) and Gervase's three uncles. We also signed an agreement with UWA, pledging to donate the land to UWA on completion of the project, to be returned to forest and ultimately contribute to a buffer zone between the forest and the local farms.

Gervase lost no time organizing a work party that I would employ in the project. The farmers and some of their older sons from the local farms came to hear from Gervase and me about our plans. Gervase had a clique of friends with whom he had grown up, and they and their wives and children became my work crew. There was a great deal to be done. The steep hillside first had to be leveled in several spots where buildings would be erected. This involved a great deal of rock moving, including some major boulder leveraging. The entire local populace turned out for some of these chores, sometimes with enormous jugs of homemade banana beer in tow for the after-boulder-moving party.

The wood for the framework of the camp could not, of course, come from either the forest or any of the local hardwoods. But a man who lived up the valley had a grove of eucalyptus trees (a fast-growing exotic species grown for lumber and fuel) that he was willing to sell. With Bosco's help I negotiated the sale of a stand of the trees, and Gervase assured me the men in my crew would begin cutting the trees and carrying them down the mountain to the camp the following day. As I opened my tent the following morning, I saw a line of small children, most no bigger than my own five-year-old son, walking steadily down the mountain, each balancing a 15-foot tree trunk on his or her head. Behind them came a second caravan, made up of the children's mothers, also carrying the poles. I complained to Gervase that I wasn't comfortable employing women and children to do the manual labor I had expected of my field assistants and myself. In return I got a polite verbal lecture from Gervase on how African gender roles operate, and why it would have been inappropriate for my men to do work that their wives and children could do just as well.

Meanwhile, the posts and beams had to be laid out and the frame built (Figure 3–4). A carpenter in the nearest village was hard at work on the

Figure 3–4 The research camp was constructed entirely of natural, locally available materials.

wooden doors and windows (which were to be simple wooden shutters covering framed openings in the mud huts). Once the frame was up, the villagers arrived once again to apply a plastered wall of mud to the structures. We had decided to build four buildings: a large *banda* (roofed building open on all sides) to serve as dining area cum communal room, a small kitchen behind it, and two residence houses: one for me or other visiting researchers and one for the long-term expatriate field assistant I hoped to hire. Gervase, Evarist, and any other local person who worked with us would continue to live in their own homes nearby.

The final piece of this puzzle was to find someone to run the project in my absence. I had already conducted two lengthy field studies, one in Bangladesh and another in Tanzania, and with a full-time university job and three growing children, I was limited to trips of a few weeks or months during summers and sabbatical semesters to come to Bwindi. Michele Goldsmith was completing her own Ph.D. and beginning postdoctoral work with me, but she was also a young lecturer teaching full time in the United States. Gervase seemed an able person to run the project, and was rapidly learning both the ways of the forest and the use of various electronic gadgets used in our work. But I wanted someone with a university education and a background in forestry and primate study who could help train and supervise the other assistants and also provide some intellectual leadership on-site. I posted an advertisement on an Internet site devoted to primate study opportunities, seeking someone to make a one-year commitment to be employed by me to live in a remote part of Uganda in primitive conditions. It was a semi-volunteer position: no salary, just a basic living stipend plus round-trip airfare. A ticket to a major adventure, as I put it in the ad.

The winner of this ticket to adventure was a quiet young Canadian man, Mitchell Keiver, who proved to be an ideal choice. Mitch had already spent a year as a field research assistant studying lowland gorilla in central Africa with a colleague of mine. His supervisor there had in fact been Alastair McNeilage, who was now in Bwindi running ITFC. Mitch and I met at London's Heathrow Airport in June 1997 as we both changed planes for the trip to Uganda. We bonded immediately; his dry, laconic wit, efficient style, and sense of humor made me feel comfortable around him. We were soon hiking the hills of Bwindi, where he showed that he was in excellent physical shape, and also hit it off well with Gervase. Over the ensuing months, through good times and bad, Mitch, Gervase and Evarist became a team I could rely on to carry out the project in good order.

EARLY RESULTS

By mid-1998 the project had come together; the camp was almost completed, Mitch had arrived to work with Gervase, and Bosco was settled in Ruhija to collect data on the gorilla group. I had also managed to find some funding from the Wenner Gren Foundation for Anthropological Research in New York for Bosco to enroll for his Ph.D. at Makerere University, with some courses to be taken during a semester at USC. He was hard at work following the Kyagurilo gorilla around Ruhija, and those animals were becoming more approachable every day.

Nkuringo camp was meanwhile up and running, and Mitch and Gervase were going to the forest every day to find and observe chimpanzees. The terrain made travel slow and observation infrequent, and we knew that just habituating the chimpanzees to human observers would be a multiyear effort.

I left Mitch in charge in mid-1998, and from then on I received regular e-mail reports of goings-on in Nkuringo. Gervase and Mitch educated each other, and the two of them worked to improve Evarist's camp-keeping skills. On my last visit to the camp during 1997, as we sat drinking tea in the gathering dusk, we heard singing high on the mountainside. A group of local ladies was parading down from the villages, across the terraced farmland, heading for our camp. They arrived and began a rhythmic group dance

Figure 3–5 When the camp was completed, women from the local village came to welcome us with a traditional dance.

line that featured frequent graceful jumping, and much highly emotional singing (Figure 3–5). We recognized some of the women as those who had helped build the camp. This was, according to Gervase, a formal welcome for us to their community. The happiness and tranquility of that evening seemed hard to recall given the events that were to follow.

4

Paradise Lost

By the end of 1998, BIGAPE was finally up and running smoothly. We had conducted enough survey work in Nkuringo Valley to know some basic parameters of the chimpanzee community there. Bosco was in his second full year collecting data on the Ruhija gorilla group on the other side of the park, and I was working to find him sponsorship and funding to conduct his Ph.D., which would make him the first African national to receive a doctorate while studying mountain gorillas. Michele Goldsmith had finished her initial postdoctoral work on the gorillas and had switched her focus to the effects of tourism on gorilla health, which led her to move her work to the tourism center at Buhoma. But the camp at Nkuringo was finished, and Camp Kashasha, as we named it, was beautiful (Figures 4–1, 4–2). The tiny camp was visible from kilometers away, bordered on one side by the Kashasha River, only a hundred meters or so away down a steep slope. The other side of the camp sloped steeply upward to a small village and dirt road an hour's walk away. Beyond that road lay the Democratic Republic of Congo, only a few kilometers away across rolling hills and emerald-green farmland.

The camp was finally in full swing as I arrived in January 1999 to spend a month in the field with the field assistants. Mitch Keiver had prospered during his months in Nkuringo; his house was a neat mud-brick bungalow fronted by a flower garden, with a panoramic view of the valley and forest. The central banda had evolved into a communal kitchen and dining room. Evarist had developed from an eager but unskilled local helper to a chef—trained from the Peace Corps cookbook Mitch had provided—and camp

Figure 4–1 Nkuringo camp at a distance; notice the sharp break between the dense forest of the national park at left and the deforested farmland to the right.

Figure 4–2 The camp kitchen and communal dining hut.

keeper. He also continued to fill in as forest field assistant when needed. The camp had a hot shower of sorts—a campers' bladder of heated water suspended over a rattan shower stall—with a view of the forest all around. In general, I was extremely pleased with the results of three years' efforts to get the project rolling and build the camp.

I spent the month hiking around the forest at Nkuringo with Mitch and Gervase looking for chimpanzees and gorillas, and only occasionally getting near them. The evenings were spent around the table in the banda talking and listening to the BBC news on the shortwave radio. Among the many news stories we listened to were reports of some border incursions along the Uganda–Congo border, in an area some 50 kilometers from Bwindi. These incursions were carried out by presumed Rwandan rebels, the infamous Interahamwe. These were the militias of Hutu extremists who carried out the genocide of Tutsi in Rwanda several years earlier, in 1994. Following the latest in Rwanda's frequent civil wars, government troops had driven the Interahamwe out of Rwanda into the Democratic Republic of Congo. There, it was thought they had drifted into the local population and had become impoverished villagers and farmers. Now we began to hear that small groups of people were making nighttime raids across the border into Uganda, pillaging villages and stealing weapons, supplies, and food.

Mitch and I listened with only moderate interest to these reports. Although we were a stone's throw from the Congo border, there had been no history of such trouble in the Bwindi area. The U.S. State Department, which always errs on the side of extreme caution in its reports on security in other countries, had issued no warning about the Bwindi area either. Besides, as Mitch and I said to each other more than once, how could a little ragtag group of ex-rebels be dumb enough to attack a tourist camp full of armed guards and rangers? We felt that our own little camp, about a five-hour hike into the forest from the tourism camp at Buhoma, was safe simply because of its location and the improbability that anyone with bad intentions would even know we were here. My family and friends at home have worried about my safety living and working in remote corners of the developing world, sometimes in areas prone to political instability or natural disasters. I've always reassured them that, in general, one is more safe in the rural third world than in any American city. Rural Africa is not so different from rural America. Everybody knows everybody, strangers are immediately identifiable, and people tend to look out for and help one another.

As it turned out, even as Mitch and I spoke these words of mutual reassurance, plans were bring laid by a Rwandan rebel militia for a bold attack on the camp at Buhoma. Days after that attack, it would be reported that a man had been seen walking around the tourist camp, making notes on the locations of the warden's office, the luxury tourist tented camps, and other buildings. Rumor has it that he was Ugandan, and hatched a plan that he sold to Interahamwe across the border. The motive for the ensuing attack, widely reported in the international media as political (to embarrass Uganda and its British and American allies) was likely more simple banditry, with any other mayhem a secondary goal.

During the last week of February, Mitch and I and porters packed up and we hiked out of the camp to Buhoma. After spending a night there, we left on the six-hour drive to Kampala in Mitch's new Suzuki jeep. Mitch was nearing the end of his contract with me and had been offered a position with the International Gorilla Conservation Programme (IGCP), a wing of the outstanding conservation organization African Wildlife Foundation. The vehicle was to become his IGCP transportation. We had a final beer at the venerable Speke Hotel in Kampala, and I saw him off that night before catching my flight back to Los Angeles. Our last bit of conversation consisted of Mitch giving me a summary of his itinerary—he had a few things to take care of before heading back to Buhoma and hiking back out to Nkuringo.

I changed planes in London and arrived in Los Angeles on February 26, tired and jet-lagged as always, but happy to be home with my wife and children. The following night, I was going through my backlog of e-mail correspondence when a message popped in from a colleague who was running the mountain gorilla project at Karisoke in Rwanda. Her e-mail was succinct: "I've just heard that there has been an Interahamwe attack at Buhoma Camp at Bwindi, maybe a robbery of some kind. Don't have any other details but will keep you posted." I did not think too much of it at the time, as information in remote places tends to be sketchy and any attack at Buhoma would not directly affect our project in the forest many kilometers away.

The next morning, on the 28th, I was sitting down to a family breakfast when the phone rang. A woman identified herself as an official of the Canadian Foreign Affairs Office in Ottawa. She asked me if Mitchell Keiver (who was a Canadian citizen) was my employee, and told me he had been kidnapped and was being held hostage in Uganda. I explained that there must be a mistake; Mitch had not been at the camp or even in Bwindi that day according to the itinerary he had given me, so he certainly could not have been among the kidnapping victims. She then said she had confirmed information, that he was in fact a hostage and that she had been in touch with Mitch's family in Alberta, Canada, who told her he had changed his itinerary after I had left and so was in the tourist camp on the day of the attack.

I immediately called Mitch's mother in Alberta. The Keiver family lives on a large farm outside Calgary. I had never met her, but from Mitch's descriptions the Keivers seemed to have a fairly idyllic small-town life. I was not looking forward to the conversation. Mrs. Keiver and I spoke only briefly, filling each other in on the facts as we knew them. I wanted badly to reassure her, but how does one reassure someone whose son has been kidnapped by people who had already massacred nearly a million people a few years earlier? The prospects for Mitch surviving did not seem promising. As it turned out, 13 foreign nationals, including Mitch, had been kidnapped from the camp that fateful morning, eight of whom ultimately died; 17 others had hidden in the forest or otherwise escaped their assailants. In addition, the warden in charge of community conservation, Paul Wagaba, had been brutally murdered. The attack had come at dawn, and Mitch had spent the night in one of the simple tourists huts in the community campground near the entrance to the park. After making a diversionary attack on the nearby town of Butagota (which is on the Congo border, presumably where the attackers crossed into Uganda unseen), a rebel militia of more than one hundred men marched down the entrance road to Buhoma, taking it completely by surprise.

The rebels overwhelmed the camp and, after setting fire to tourist lodges and cars and robbing the camps, headed into the densely forested hills with their hostages. The forced march took them toward the border with Congo, where after some intense negotiation between hostages and hostage-takers, one group was released. This group included Mitch. After 24 agonizing hours, I received a call from the head of the U.S. Information Service in Kampala, telling me that Mitch was safe. Other foreigners were less fortunate; the rebels left a trail of murdered bodies as they fled back across the border. Before being evacuated by plane back to Kampala and, a week later, home to Canada, Mitch made arrangements to rescue the camp dog, Peppie, had been stranded alone when all the human residents of Camp Kashasha fled (and now resides on the Keiver farm in Alberta).

With Mitch safe, our thoughts turned to whether it would be possible to continue the study. In the first few days and weeks, that seemed almost moot. But the UPDF, Uganda's military force, beefed up their presence in the park immediately after the attack, and within a few months it seemed clear that both tourism and research would return. The fragile balance between tourist revenue and gorilla conservation had been badly damaged by the attacks. In 1998 and the early weeks of 1999, gorilla-tracking permits were a hot commodity at Bwindi, with long waiting lists for those who showed up at Buhoma without a prebooked spot on a trek. Following the attacks and the closure of nearly all the major tourist lodges, gorilla tourism virtually disappeared. That summer, normally the peak of the tourist season, Buhoma was a quiet place. But by late 1999, with improved security and a highly publicized tourist visit to the gorillas by Ugandan president Yoweri Museveni, the tourists began to trickle back. First came the independent backpackers, never known for any lack of pluck, and then chartered tour groups of high-rolling foreigners began to return as well.

During this period, the director of the ITFC, the nongovernmental organization that administered research in Bwindi, was Richard Malenky.

Richard was a veteran of many field projects in remote places, and he and his wife, Nancy Thompson-Handler, were voices of reason when many felt it was too dangerous to continue the BIGAPE project. Richard and I agreed that it was an unreasonable risk to continue to run the project from the camp in Nkuringo valley, but that the project needed to continue. We worked out a plan to shift the project's base of operation from Nkuringo Valley to the existing research headquarters at Ruhija. Ruhija, some forty kilometers across the park in the opposite direction from the Congo border, was inherently more secure from future attacks, and the lone dirt road that accessed the research station was to be protected henceforth by the UPDF. The ITFC station was situated on top of one of the highest points in the park at about 2,300 meters elevation; the mountaintop had been leveled off and a camp of several rustic buildings had been constructed in the 1980s. We traded the autonomy, isolation, and panoramic beauty of the camp at Nkuringo for the security and logistical convenience of Ruhija. Ruhija came complete with a cataloged collection of plants for identification (later enlarged to a beautiful field herbarium by Richard's successor, Alastair McNeilage), plus an excellent library. In the evening, there was a view from the lawn of the main house of the Virunga Volcanoes some 25 kilometers away.

At Ruhija we would also have new, additional personnel to help with the study. There was a botanical expert on staff, Robert Barygera, and a team of more than a dozen field assistants. We would work in rotating teams of two men per day. The presence of Bosco and the ITFC assistants enabled us to increase human observer contact time with the new chimpanzee community.

In Nkuringo we had interviewed and selected local villagers, whom Mitch then trained as field assistants over many months. Gervase had come to me as the younger brother of a senior park ranger, and the land on which Camp Kashasha stood was purchased from his uncles. Gervase's home was in Nkuringo, where he had farm plots, a young wife, and two young children. The move to Ruhija created a dilemma for him; either stay with his family farm and lose employment income that is very hard to come by in rural Africa, or move with the project and be separated from his wife and children for weeks at a time. In the end, Gervase chose to come with us to Ruhija, and we worked out a plan in which he saved up his off time from work and took off several days at the end of each month, when he made the trip to his home village. In later years the project purchased a motorcycle for him to make this trip much easier.

The other field assistants stayed in Nkuringo. Evarist, our cook and camp keeper, later worked as a field assistant for Michele Goldsmith's tourism project in Nkuringo. Paul, Jack, Christophe, and the others who had built the camp went back to their pre-research lives. Under the terms by which we had been allowed to purchase the land bordering the park in

Nkuringo, once the project was done with the land it was to be deeded to the Uganda Wildlife Authority, which had had designs on the possibilities for ecotourism in Nkuringo for years. A tourist camp was planned for the Nkuringo area, just a few minutes walk from our land. The land on which our camp stood was, by general agreement, going to be donated to UWA to become part of a narrow buffer zone between the forest itself and the broad expanse of hilly farmland just outside the park.

The camp itself quickly returned to the forest. Once we had set ourselves up in Ruhija and it was clear we would no longer use the camp even on a temporary basis, I gave permission to some of our local friends to take furniture, window and door frames, and the like. Because the camp buildings had, by agreement with UWA, been built of temporary materials—wooden frames with mud brick—it did not take long for the forest to reclaim them.

By 2000, tourists were returning to Bwindi. The fate of the gorillas, always hinged so directly to the fate of local people, began to improve. More tourists meant more tourist dollars for the local economy, which meant fewer people resentful of gorillas raiding their crops or threatening them when encountered in their fields. Before long, not only was tourism back in full swing, and luxury camps rebuilt, but Nkuringo had indeed become a center for ecotourism. Operating not far from our old camp, groups of six tourists at a time tracked the Nkuringo gorilla group and spent an hour watching them, at a fee of upwards of $300 per person. This brought money to both the people of Nkuringo, and to people farther away who came daily to sell their produce, wood carvings, and such to the foreign visitors.

The ultimate fate of Nkuringo and its apes remains to be seen. Gorillas may have become victims of their own success, with regard to habituation. Having become utterly accustomed to human observers at close range, the Nkuringo gorillas began to spend less and less time in the forest. At first this was highly desirable; it's easier to find a gorilla group sitting in a farmer's field than to trek miles into the forest to find them. But they quickly became problematic, at one point living and sleeping far from the nearest edge of the forest and national park for six months. No one wants gorillas out of the forest. For local farmers, they wreak havoc with crops, tearing apart banana plantations; the several farmers who accidentally stumbled across silverbacks sleeping in the grass received rude shocks, too, although the charges the apes made on farmers were generally bluffs.

For the park rangers, monitoring and protecting the gorillas as they wandered freely from village to village meant trying to diplomatically shepherd them away from houses and population centers. The rangers tried using bells, whistles, and at one point blasts from air horns to drive them back to the forest, all to no avail. Once their fear of people was gone, the gorillas were smart enough to see that all this forest foraging was nonsense; good food was to be had in quantity and gotten with ease on farms and plantations. And there are major health risks to gorillas that spend time around human habitations: toxic trash that may be eaten, human parasites and infections that can be picked up, and so on.

As difficult as this situation was for the park staff, it was potentially a tourism nightmare. Tourists who travel all the way from western countries and pay $300 an hour to see the gorillas expect a wilderness experience, albeit a comfortable one. Watching majestic silverbacks reposing in a local cornfield was not going to sit well with tourists. It took some time for local tourism officials to see this. Eventually, the gorillas moved back into the forest, although as of 2005 they were still spending substantial time outside it.

The long-term impact of tourism is overall an enormous boon to the survival of the gorillas, simply because it gives the government a strong incentive to protect their future. But the political instability of the region, combined with the risks to gorilla health from tourism, will always present a double-edged sword to the future of Bwindi gorillas.

5

A New Beginning

In January 2000, we reopened the project after the nine-month hiatus brought on by the rebel attack of March 1, 1999. The camp we had lovingly constructed at Nkuringo was abandoned, its mud and wood buildings quickly returning to the forest. Following the international attention over the murders of the ecotourists, the Ugandan government increased its military presence in Bwindi, and the security situation improved greatly. The ecotourism camp at Buhoma became a center of military activity, with a barracks and many troops stationed there. At one point a tank was wheeled into the camp; whether it was functional or not, it apparently was thought a tank would give pause to any future attackers. Checkpoints were set up on all access roads. Slowly, tourists began returning. First came the intrepid backpackers and overland truckers, and later the main luxury ecotour companies came back and reestablished themselves at Buhoma.

We waited several months to see if it would be possible to return to Bwindi and reestablish the field project. Eventually we decided to go ahead and restart the project; the security situation seemed calm and other scientists were coming back to work on other projects. Bosco was ready to begin collecting data for his doctoral thesis, and the field assistants were happy to be employed again. However, I decided that because the Kashasha camp was located only a few kilometers from the international border with Congo, we could never feel safe in that site again. I could not risk the lives of students or field assistants (or my family, who had been scheduled to make an extended visit) who might become victims of another attack. So the decision was made to move the study to Ruhija, a site on the other side of the park that was already the formal research headquarters for all other Bwindi research projects. Ruhija is a very different habitat from Nkuringo: about 500–700 meters higher in elevation, a more rugged and hilly place that resembles the Virunga Volcanoes. Ruhija offered a logistically advantageous, seemingly safe place to work, and with the approval of the park administrators, I moved the work there beginning in January 2000.

RUHIJA CHIMPANZEES AND GORILLAS

In every setback there is supposed to be a silver lining. This was true in ours, because reestablishing the project in another part of the park led us to set up a new chimpanzee study in the same area where Bosco had already been studying his well-habituated gorilla group since 1997. This group, locally known as the Kyagurilo gorillas or simply "the research group," had been somewhat shy of people at the time of my first visit to Ruhija in 1996. By 1998 the team of Ugandan field assistants plus Bosco had habituated the gorillas to the point that researchers could approach the animals closely to gather detailed observational data on their behavior. Since the research gorillas lived in a part of the park that was almost fifty kilometers away from the scene of the attack, and also many kilometers from the Congo border, Bosco's work had continued almost uninterrupted following the rebel incursion. Now we would abandon habituation and observation of the Nkuringo chimpanzees and would habituate and study a new community in the Ruhija area.

This move ultimately proved extremely fortuitous. Not only was there a diverse primate community (Table 5–1), there were many chimpanzees living in Ruhija. The "Ruhija chimpanzees" occupied almost precisely the same home range as the Kyagurilo research gorilla group. In nearly the same 22-square-kilometer patch of forest lived a community of at least 26 chimpanzees, the research gorilla group (consisting of thirteen members

Table 5–1 The Diurnal Primate Community of Ruhija Study Site

Common Name	Scientific Name	Note
Chimpanzee	*Pan troglodytes schweinfurthii*	community of 26¹
Gorilla	*Gorilla gorilla beringei*	2 groups, 21¹ total
Red-tailed guenon	*Cercopithecus ascanius schmidti*	low density
Blue guenon	*Cercopithecus mitis mitis*	low density
L'Hoest's guenon	*Cercopithecus l'hoesti*	semiterrestrial
Vervet	*Cercopithecus aethiops*	mainly fields
Savanna baboon	*Papio anubis*	mainly fields
Black-and-white colobus	*Colobus guereza abyssinicus*	common

in January 2000), another gorilla group that was not habituated, plus the occasional lone silverback. The density of gorillas and chimpanzees in the study site was roughly the same, one ape per square kilometer. This situation allowed us, over subsequent years, to study the relationship between the chimpanzees and gorillas and their habitat knowing that both species had exactly the same access to the same resources, with the same habitat constraints, such as elevation, temperature, and rainfall. Instead of studying sympatric apes that were only broadly sympatric within the same national park, we were studying the two species in an area in which they not only overlapped fully in range, but might occasionally bump into each other. We were very eager to know how often this happened, and what the outcome of such encounters would be.

The other silver lining of the shift in location involved the chimpanzees themselves. Nkuringo's terrain had been so steep and rugged that approaching the chimpanzees to accustom them to our presence had been nearly impossible. Although we had good information about their diet, we knew very little about their social behavior: dominance, mother–infant, male–female relations, and all the other social dynamics of the community. At Ruhija, researchers were allowed to establish overnight campsites in other pristine forest. This allowed the field assistants and us to sleep near the feeding trees chimpanzees were using, and arrive early enough the next morning to catch them before they awakened in their nests.

Almost as soon as we moved to Ruhija, the field assistants began making contact with the chimpanzees. Primates can, like people, be shy or bold. The Ruhija community may have contained a few bold males, or perhaps they were already accustomed to seeing researchers hiking on forest trails. We were able to assemble a fairly complete picture of the chimpanzees' identity in the community within the first year. We were not able to approach at close range as we could with the gorillas, and could not follow chimpanzees on the ground because of the dense undergrowth, and the ensuing crashing noises as we tried to get through thickets to approach them.

We could, however, approach quietly and sit within plain sight of trees in which the new chimpanzees were feeding. This proved to be the most effective way of both habituating and observing them. When we knew where the chimpanzees were feeding—in a large fig tree, for example—we would hike to the tree early in the morning and sit quietly near it until the chimpanzees appeared. Massive figs of several species were scattered through the forest, and when in fruit they became moveable feasts for chimpanzees, gorillas, monkeys, birds, and other animals. The feeding frenzy no doubt continued through the nighttime hours too, when nocturnal animals such as fruit bats and palm civets would arrive. These trees were essential to our ability to watch our chimpanzees, especially in the early days of the study in Ruhija. Two decades earlier, Michael Ghiglieri (1984) had undertaken a field study of similarly shy chimpanzees at Ngogo in Kibale National Park, Uganda, some 200 kilometers north of Bwindi. He had used a method he called "focal tree sampling" in which he stationed himself under trees chimpanzees were likely to come to, rather than attempting to track the shy apes. We did the same thing, with much success. Even after nine years we were not able to walk behind the chimpanzees or approach them on foot while they were on the ground. But they did not mind at all having us sitting 20 to 50 meters away in plain sight as they fed in trees.

The most exciting aspect of the new study venue was the possibility of seeing both chimpanzees and gorillas together. Although this had been observed occasionally in western and central Africa, no one had even seen mountain gorillas and chimpanzees in the same trees. Would they share food amicably or compete over it? If they competed, which species would prove to be ecologically and behaviorally dominant? Since the two apes in Ruhija shared exactly the same resource base, what were the differences in resource use? What were the social dynamics during encounters between the two species? We had a lot of unanswered questions, and as the project progressed in Ruhija, we were able to begin providing answers.

A NEW CAST OF CHARACTERS

During the first several months of field research in Ruhija, we learned as much about the local chimpanzees as we had learned in three years in Nkuringo (Table 5–2). The full and exact memberships of chimpanzee communities are notoriously difficult to know, because the animals do not live in cohesive groups the way gorillas do. There are typically an assortment of adult and adolescent males who spend much of their time together, plus female and their younger offspring who associate with the males when it suits them. Some young adult males travel alone as well. Consequently, chimpanzee researchers typically learn the identities and social dynamics of males long before that of females. To further complicate things, until you know the exact range boundaries of the chimpanzee community— their territory—it's impossible to be certain the chimpanzees you are seeing are from "your" community or a neighboring one.

We quickly identified a chimpanzee community in Ruhija that consisted of at least 26 animals. Mboneire (which we abbreviated MB; "handsome" in Ruchiga language) was a very handsome adult male in his prime, with thick jet-black hair. It quickly became apparent that Mboneire was the alpha— top-ranking—male. We based this on the pattern of submissive vocalizations and body language made toward him by other males, combined with his own displays of dominance. When Mboneire arrived in a fruit-laden tree crown, other males gave way, allowing him to sit where he chose. When a skirmish broke out among the chimpanzees, Mboneire would launch a display with impunity, telling the others they would be well advised to settle

Table 5–2 Identities of Chimpanzees and Gorillas in Ruhija during Study Period

Chimpanzees (Ruhija community)

Name	Sex	Age	Notes
Mboneire	M	AD	Alpha
Kidevu	M	AD	Intermediate rank
Kushoto	M	AD	Low rank
Frodo	M	AD	Intermediate/high rank
Julius	M	SubAd	Low rank
Yower	M	SubAd	Low rank
Martha	F	AD	Mother of May (MY)
Faida	F	AD	Mother of Furaha (FU)
Kampala	F	AD	Mother of Kenya (KY)
Patches	F	AD	Mother of Pachouli (PC)
Unnamed	F	AD	Peripheral; Mother of infant

(Plus at least three other adult females seen irregularly and believed to be peripheral members of the community)

Name	Sex	Age	Notes
Innocent	M	JUV	Male about 5–6 years old in 2000
Unnamed	F	JUV	Female about 7 years old in 2000

Gorillas (Kyagurilo group)

Name	Sex	Age	Notes
Zeuss	M	?	Silverback through 2004
Rukina	M	AD	Became silverback in 2003–04
Nteganisa	M	AD	Emigrated in 1999
Marembo	M	SubAd	
Sikio	M	SubAd	
Byiza	M	SubAd	
Fuzi	M	JUV/SubAd	
Binyindo	F	AD	Mother of Thursday
Siatu	F	AD	
Matu	F	AD	
Tinamanyire	F	AD	Mother of Kabindize
Kakumu	F	AD	
Mugwere	F	AD	Mother of Happy
Bizibu	F	JUV	
Mukiza	M	JUV	
Kabandize	M	INF	
Thursday	?	INF	
Happy	?	INF	

down. The other males groomed Mboneire far more often than he returned the favor. Recording this pattern of interactions over time showed a clear dominance status, but it was obvious to anyone who sat for a few hours watching the community.

Kidevu (KD; "bearded" in Kiswahili) was an older male with a white-bearded chin. The fingers of his right hand were somewhat deformed; he held them stiffly erect when grasping food. The Bwindi chimpanzees were extremely fortunate not to be as severely victimized by poachers' snares as other chimpanzee populations in Uganda. Indeed, in forests such as Kibale National Park and Budongo Forest Reserve to the north of Bwindi, more than a third of the chimpanzees bear disabilities, including amputations, as a result of snares. The snares, typically placed in the forest to catch antelope or wild pigs, ensnare a chimpanzee's hand or foot while walking on the forest floor. In past times, the snares were made of natural fibers and would eventually decompose. Today they are more often made of metal wire, and will tighten on the wrist or ankle over time, with resulting disability or loss of the limb. Kidevu was one of only two Ruhija chimpanzees we saw who bore the wound of an old snare, and it fortunately did not seem to hamper his activities much at all. Kidevu was a male of intermediate rank, a submissive ally to Mboneire.

The other male who bore a snare injury was the low-ranking Kushoto (KU; "left" in Kiswahili). The skin and facial complexions of chimpanzees vary widely, as do those of people. Kushoto had a red freckled face, a white chin, and brown (instead of black) hair on his back. His right wrist and hand were stiff and deformed, and a wire snare hung visibly from it. This did not seem to impair his ability to climb or feed, however. Kushoto was a low-ranking adult who was almost always seen in the company of Kidevu. Such consistent alliances sometimes are connected to kinship, and the two males bore a facial resemblance. But without genetic evidence (which we did not have), they could just as easily have been unrelated, long-term allies. The last of the four fully adult males was Frodo (FR; named for the famed chimpanzee in Goodall's field study, whom our FR resembled). Frodo was a very large, prime-age male with very brown body hair, and prominent sideburns of brown tinged with silver. Unlike Gombe's Frodo, who was noted for his belligerent demeanor, our Bwindi Frodo was a huge but gentle chimpanzee. He was of medium to high rank, and although we did not know his age, we considered him to be a future powerful male in the Ruhija community.

The community also had two males who were not quite fully adult. Preadolescent male chimpanzees often pass through a life stage in which they are not very social, often traveling alone. They seem to be in between the early-life security of their mothers and the security of the adult male hierarchy. On reaching adolescence they begin to travel more often with the adults, and attempt to take their place in hunting, patrolling, and other typical male activities. In our community two males, Julius and Yoweri, occupied this status. Julius (named after Julius Nyerere, first president of modern Tanzania) was a lean, ruddy-faced male probably about fourteen to fifteen years old, and just taking his place among the adults in 2000. Yoweri (named after Yoweri Museveni, the president of Uganda), was a small adolescent male, jet-black in body hair and face, whose lower lip hung open (a common, presumably genetic trait in chimpanzees).

The Ruhija community contained five adult females. Martha (named in honor of Martha Robbins, an American researcher studying gorilla social behavior in Bwindi) was a female with a white chin. Her tendency to stand and feed in a two-legged posture was noteworthy, and she appeared to be high-ranking, though measures of rank among females are fewer and more subtle than the frequent displacements and pant grunts done by males. Martha had an infant, May (MY), who was a newborn when we first encountered them in 2000. Faida (FD; "reward" in Kiswahili) was an older, small-bodied female easily recognized by her heavily freckled, bony face and white chin. She may have suffered a long-healed injury to her right hand, which at times seems to be stiffly held and used less in favor of her right hand. Faida had a son, Furaha (FU; "happiness" in Kiswahili), who was estimated to be one to two years old in 2000.

Kampala (KM; the largest city in Uganda) was a prime-age female, all black and without any clear identifying marks except a very high, V-shaped forehead. Her infant, Kenya (KY), was a newborn in 2000. Patches (PA) was a female missing hair on each shoulder—we thought at first she was suffering from a temporary skin condition, but the appearance lasted for five years, only on the shoulders. She was in her prime and had a male infant, Patchouli (PC), who was two to three years old in 2000. One other adult female was part of the community but was not seen regularly. We called her Female 5, and she had a baby of unknown sex who was about one year old in 2000. Still other females turned up now and then, usually stalking timidly at the out-skirts of a foraging party. Because of the fluid nature of chimpanzee communities, it is hard to know their home community. These may have been peripheral members of the Ruhija community, or occasional visitors from a neighboring one. Or they may have been females who "belonged" to more than one community, and passed easily through both.

In addition to the adults and adolescents, there were two juvenile animals that were, in 2000, passing through the gray area of preadolescence described above. Innocent was a juvenile male, probably five to six years old in 2000, and Juve was a juvenile female, six or seven years old, who was often seen near Faida and could have been her daughter. By 2005, both these animals were adolescents and were spending more and more time in the company of the rest of the community (Table 5–3).

Table 5–3 Approximate Chimpanzee and Gorilla Age Categories

Chimpanzees

Neonate	Newborn infant up to 2–3 months. Tiny and held to mother's chest.
Infant 1	Infant older than neonate but less than about 1 year. Carried under mother or against her chest; rarely moves far from mother.
Infant 2	Older infant that usually rides on mother's back, and travels away from mother at times. About 1–4 years.
Juvenile	Immature that travels independently at all times, may spend time near mother, but not necessarily. About 5–9 years old.
Subadult	Large immature that travels with and acts like an adult, but smaller body size and lacks visible nipples if female. Subadult males are often alone. About 10–14 years old.
Adult Female	Obvious nipples, cycles, and swells. Above about age 13–14.
Adult Male	Above about age 15.

Gorillas

Neonate	Newborn infant up to about 3 months. Dependent on mother and carried by her.
Infant	From about 3 months to four years. Progressively more independent, but nurses from mother and returns to her in case of danger.
Juvenile	From about 4 to 8 years. Baby travels independently at all times, may spend time near mother, but not necessarily.
Subadult	Between about 9 and 15 (depending on the onset of sexual maturity, which varies among individuals and between sexes).
Adult	For females, from about age 12 on; for males, from about age 15.

The Ruhija gorillas were the same group Bosco had been studying since 1997 (see Chapter 2). In January 2000, as the project reopened, the group consisted of 13 individuals, including the same silverback male—Zeuss—plus two blackback males, Rukina and Nteganisa. Zeuss was a strong silverback, although somewhat shy about human observers and constantly attentive, as silverbacks should be, to the movements of his females. In 2000, Nteganisa was a teenager, sexually mature but socially subordinate to Zeuss. He had become a peripheral group member, trailing the other members by some distance as they moved and feeding apart from them. During the study period he ultimately emigrated, and despite repeated searches by the field assistants, his eventual whereabouts were never discovered. Rukina was a bit younger than Nteganisa, and underwent the same peripheralization from about 2003 onward. The fates of Rukina and Zeuss will be discussed in detail in Chapter 8.

PROFILING THE FOREST—PHENOLOGY

Since ecologically oriented primate field studies concern the influence of the environment on the animal, the first step in establishing such a study is understanding the plant resources. The forest trees and plants that form the diet of chimpanzees and gorillas can be analyzed for distribution (where they are located on the landscape), for abundance of particular species, and for nutritional content. The best way to sample the range of vegetation in the forest and estimate its abundance and distribution is to set up *phenological transects*. *Phenology* is the study of the forest's seasonal and annual cycles of leafing, flowering, and fruiting—its natural rhythms. It can be a central element of a primate field study, but has been neglected in many of the most important long-term studies of chimpanzees and gorillas. This is a disappointing oversight, because grouping patterns—so ephemeral and hard to predict in chimpanzees—are determined in part by the availability of foods. Failure to monitor forest cycles in some systematic way leaves researchers probing each other's memories ("Does anyone remember how big the crop of *Syzigium* was two years ago?") in hopes of understanding what accounts for this year's grouping patterns.

Transects are predetermined lines along which the vegetation is studied. For example, you might stand in the middle of the apes' home range and, using a compass to stay on a straight-line bearing, walk three kilometers, marking the trail as you go. You could then record the identity of each large tree (typically only trees over a certain trunk diameter are used) within ten meters each side of the trail.

Since it's impossible to census the thousands of trees in a forest the size of Ruhija, we use a small sample to represent the total. It's not a truly random sample, for two reasons. First, we don't want the transect to run through, for example, a swamp or pond that the gorillas and chimpanzees obviously would not use. And although one would ideally set a compass bearing and walk it, cutting a transect and marking trees as you go, this is not practical in the rugged terrain of Bwindi. Instead we used existing trails, which is not ideal in that they may have been chosen for a reason that might bias the trees found in the transect. An easy slope for hiking, for instance, might be a good choice for trail-making but a poor choice for a transect. But the use of existing trails, at least in Bwindi, outweighs any potential downside. The transect does not need to be cut, which saves a swath of forest from damage from cutting and repeated foot travel.

Trails snake their way through Bwindi, some of them tens of kilometers long. We chose the two main trails that bisected the study site at Ruhija. The longer one, Nyaruchundura, ran from the dirt road that encircles the study site down a tortuously steep grade, culminating some two kilometers and three hundred meters elevation below. It ran into Mubwindi Swamp, at 2,000 meters elevation the highest swamp in East Africa and a place of great ecological importance because of the number of rare bird species breeding there. On the far side of the swamp, the transect continued for some distance up into the hilly forest. The other trail, Kajembejembe, was shorter, only about three kilometers from the same road head to the swamp, and also less steeply sloped.

There are a variety of habitat types within the forest at Ruhija. Most of the forest is a mixture of *Chrysophyllum*-dominated open or mixed forest. Small areas of mature primary forest exist (Bwindi was logged selectively during British colonial times), as well as stands of montane forest and swamp. Bamboo (*Arundinaria alpina*, Poaceae), which makes up more than half of mountain gorilla habitat in the nearby Virunga Volcanoes, is a rare plant in Bwindi, occurring in abundance only on the highest ridges of the park.

Once the transects have been established, it's time to identify and record the trees. All trees having a trunk diameter at least nine centimeters at chest height and standing within five meters either side of the transects were included. Naming the trees is easy for some of our local field assistants; they grew up in and around the forest and know each tree the way you might know the maples and oaks in your backyard. The problem is that we need to know the botanical names for the plants, and local people sometimes have their own categories that don't fit our plant taxonomy. For instance, there were a number of enormous figs in the study site, in the genus *Ficus* (Family Moraceae). Fig taxonomy is notoriously confused and has undergone recent major revisions (Herre et al. 1996). But local names for our Ruhija figs added a whole new layer of confusion. The local (Ruchiga language) name for *Ficus sur* (formerly known to botanists as *F. capensis*) is *Echitoma*. But *Echitoma* is also applied to other figs, such as *F. natalensis* and *F. vallis-choudae*. Unlike most trees, which are bisexual and produce both male and female flowers, most figs are dioecious, with different trees of each sex occurring. Local names were given to males and females as though these were separate species. Bwindi has a good field herbarium, where specimens of each plant are stored for reference purposes, as well as a very good herbarist, Robert Borygera. Even so, in the end we decided to refer to the figs you will read about here as the generic *Ficus sp.* to avoid any mistaken identification labels.

We placed metal tags and orange flagging on 174 trees in Ruhija, with a supplemental transect maintained in Nkuringo in the preattack study site. This is a small number compared to studies conducted in lowland tropical forests, where the diversity of tree species is far greater. The goal is to have ten individuals of each important food species marked and monitored in the transects; this can mean transects of five hundred trees marked in some sites (for example, Doran & McNeilage 1998). We had 35 species in our sample of 174, which included nearly all of the important food tree species used by chimpanzees, gorillas, or both. Even so, keeping track of the lives of 174 trees required several days' work each month by the field assistants. In practice, keeping phenological records meant walking the transect the same three or four days of each month to record whether trees had, for example, ripe or unripe fruit. The same field assistant—Gervase, with assistance from the others—would sit under each tree and scan the crown with binoculars to see what was happening in the tree. We used abundance scales to indicate the level of fruit crop if there was one.

This monthly snapshot of the trees used by chimpanzees and gorillas plays a vital role in connecting the diet and feeding behavior of the animals to their resource base. Knowing that gorilla diet in August drops suddenly from largely fruit (in July) to largely foliage is interesting. But knowing that this dietary shift accompanies a sharp drop in the availability of fruit in the forest is a far more powerful connection, as it suggests a likely cause and effect. The real power of this information does not, however, become clear until phenological data have been recorded for years. Then it's possible to look back through the records and see patterns. Fruit abundance might, for example, show a significant positive correlation with fruit consumption, and both might be correlated with rainfall. Or, it might be related to the amount of rainfall the year prior to the observed bumper fruit crop. Moreover, some trees do not bear fruit every year, but have alternating boom-and-bust years. One tree species in our own sample was *Podocarpus milianjianus* (Podocarpaceae). This species (relatives of which are widely planted in the United States as ornamentals) was a fairly common tree in Ruhija that produced small pinkish pulpy fruits. But only after four years of phenological monitoring did we observe widespread fruiting in the species—for the first three years of phenology study, *P. milianjianus* barely produced fruit at all. The sudden bumper crop might be explained by rainfall, by natural boom-and-bust cycles, or even by a genetic adaptation that promotes irregular, synchronous fruiting. Without phenological information, it might not have been noticed.

DIET

The results of the phenological transect data were very important in understanding chimpanzee and gorilla diets. They showed that the availability of tree fruits was highly seasonal, with the quantity and diversity of fruits high from January through July, and then dropping to almost zero from August through December. At the same time, the availability of leafy foliage remained high, and as we will see in Chapter 6, gorillas turned to this diet in fruit-poor periods. These results were quite consistent from 2000 to 2005. Fruit abundance showed a peak during the dry months of September to April (Figure 5–1). The doctoral work of my Ph.D. student, Bosco (Nkurunungi 2005), showed, however, that there was no significant correlation between monthly variation in rainfall and the incidence of trees in the study site bearing either ripe fruit (Spearman R 5 2.20, p 5 .51) or any fruit at all (Spearman R 5 2.31, p 5 .17; Nkurunungi, 2005). This does not mean that fruit production did not track rainfall in some way; there could be a one-, two-, or several-year lag between rainfall and fruit abundance. But it does indicate that rainfall did not have an immediate influence on fruit production.

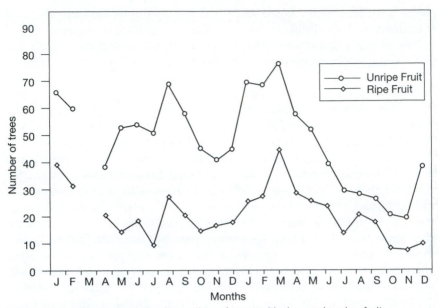

Figure 5–1 Monthly variation in number of trees with ripe and unripe fruit.
Source: From Nkurunungi 2005.

The Ruhija chimpanzees ate 60 different plant parts from at least 32 plant species, representing 26 plant families. In the same habitat, the Kyagurilo gorillas ate 133 different plant parts of at least 96 species, representing 58 plant families (Table 5–4). The chimpanzees also consumed at least two species of vertebrate animals and three species of invertebrate, while the gorillas ingested stones and decomposed wood.

Fruit was the most frequently eaten food in the chimpanzee diet, with 30 species eaten: 64.6% fruit, and 27.1% leaves plus plant shoots. Evidence of fruit-eating was found in 98.4% of fecal samples. An average of 2.1 fruit samples were found per fecal sample, with a range of from one to six species per sample.

The chimpanzees ate a wide variety of fruits, from figs filled with thousands of tiny seeds to large *Myrianthus holstii* fruits containing large pitlike seeds. Some fruits (*Syzigium guineense*, for example) were pulpy and sweet when ripe, resembling reddish grapes. Other fruits, like *Chrysophyllum sp.*, were filled with white, rubbery flesh and did not appear to be very digestible. Figs were the most abundant fruits by far in the chimpanzee diet, appearing in more than twice as many samples as the next most common fruit (*Drypetes gerrardii;* 29% vs. 14%). The seeds of the figs were also the most abundant seeds found (present in 69% of chimpanzee fecal samples). Because of confusion over their identification (both by botanists and local field assistants who refer to multiple species and different fig sexes by the same name), all our Ruhija figs were lumped together as *Ficus sp.* This

Table 5–4 Species of Plants Eaten by Bwindi Chimpanzees and Gorillas

Species/Family	Eaten by?	Pulp	Seed	Leaf	Flower	Pith
Acalypha agrogyna (Tiliaceae)	G					x
Adenia sp. (Passifloraceae)	G			x		
Allophylus macrobotrys (Sapindaceae)	G	x		x		
Allophylus sp. (Sapindaceae)	G	x				
Alchornea hirtella (Euphorbiaceae)	G/C	x		x		
Arundinaria alpina (Poaceae)	G	x		x		x
Basella alba (Basellaceae)	G			x		
Brillantasia sp. (Acanthaceae)	G			x	x	
Carapa grandiflora (Meliaceae)	C	x		x		
Cardus sp. (Compositae)	G/C			x	x	
Carpodinus glabra (Apocynaceae)	G			x		
Cassipourea sp. (Rubiaceae)	G/C			x	wood	
Chrysophyllum gorungosanum (Sapotaceae)	G/C	x	x			
Chrysophyllum albidum (Sapotaceae)	G/C	x	x			
Cissus sp. (Vitaceae)	G			x		
Clematis sp. (Ranunculiaceae)	G/C			x		
Clerodendron sp. (Verbenaceae)	G			x		
Clutia abyssinica (Euphorbiaceae)	G	x				
Coccinia bateri (Curcubitaceae)	G			x		
Coccinia mildbraedi (Curcubitaceae)	G	x		x		
Crassocephalum manni (Compositae)	G				x	
Crassocephalum rubens (Compositae)	G			x		x
Cyantheae maniana (Cyanthaceae)	G					x
Cyperus sp. (Cyperaceae)	G				x	
Desmodium repandum (Fabaceae)	G				x wood	
Desmodium sp. (Fabaceae)	G				x	x
Dicliptera sp. (Acanthaceae)	G			x		
Dombeya goetzenii (Sterculiaceae)	G			x		
Drynaria volkensii (Polypodiaceae)	G					x
Drypetes gerrardii (Euphorbiaceae)	G/C	x				
Englerina sp. (Loranthaceae)	G		x	x		
Faurea saligna (Protaceae)	G				wood	
Ficus sp. (Moraceae)	G/C	x	x	x	bark	
Ficalhoa laurifolia (Theaceae)	G				wood	
Fleurya ovalifolia (Urticaceae)	G			x		
Galiniera coffeioides (Rubiaceae)	G	x				
Galium sp. (Rubiaceae)	G			x		x
Ganoderma australe (Polyporaceae)	G				fungus	
Geranium sp. (Geraniaceae)	G			x		x

(Continued)

Table 5–4 Continued

Species/Family	Eaten by?	Pulp	Seed	Leaf	Flower	Pith
Govania longispicata (Rhaminaceae)	G			x		
Gynura sp. (Asteraceae)	G			x		
Helichrysum sp. (Compositae)	G			x		
Ipomea sp. (Convulvulaceae)	G			x	x	bark
Jasminium eminii (Oleaceae)	G/C			x		
Justicia sp. (Acanthaceae)	G			x		
Kosteletzkya grantii (Malvaceae)	G			x	x	
Landolphia buchanani (Apocynaceae)	G			x		
Langenaria sp. (Curcubitaceae)	G			x		
Laportea sp. (Urticaceae)	G			x		
Loranthus sp. (Loranthaceae)	G			x	x	
Maesa lanceolata (Myrsinaceae)	G/C	x	x		wood	
Maytenus acuminata (Celastraceae)	G				wood	
Mimulopsis sp. (Acanthaceae)	G/C			x		
Mormodica calantha (Curcubitaceae)	G/C	x		x		
Mormodica foetida (Curcubitaceae)	G/C	x		x		
Myrianthus holstii (Moraceae)	G/C	x	x		bark	
Myrica salicifolia (Myricaceae)	G				wood	
Mystroxylon aethiopica (Celastraceae)	G/C	x	x		wood	
Olea capense (Oleaceae)	G/C	x	x	x	wood	
Olinia usambarensis (Olinaceae)	G/C	x	x		wood	
Parinari holstii (Chrysobalanaceae)	G/C	x	x			x
Piper capense (Piperaceae)	G					x
Pleripoca linearifolia (Asclepidaceae)	G			x		
Podocarpus milinjianus (Podocarpaceae)	G/C	x				
Prena angolensis (Verbenaceae)	G				wood	
Prunus africana (Rosaceae)	G/C			x		
Psychotria mahonii (Rubiaceae)	G				wood	
Pycnostachys elliotti (Labitae)	G			x		
Rapennea rhodrodites (Celastraceae)	G			x	wood	
Rawnsonia lucida (Flaucourtaceae)	G/C	x				x
Rubia cordifolia (Rubiaceae)	G/C			x		x
Rubus sp. (Rosaceae)	G/C	x		x		
Rumex bequertii (Polygonaceae)	G			x		x
Rumex sp. (Polygonaceae)	G			x		
Rhytiginia beninensis (Rubiaceae)	G			x		
Rhytiginia sp. (Rubiaceae)	G	x		x		
Rhytigina ruenzoriensis (Rubiaceae)	G/C	x				
Salacia elegans (Celastraceae)	G	x		x		

Table 5–4 Continued

Species/Family	Eaten by?	Pulp	Seed	Leaf	Flower	Pith
Sapium ellipticum (Euphorbiaceae)	G/C	x			wood	
Schefflera barteri (Araliaceae)	G			x		
Sellaginela sp. (Sellaginaceae)	G			x		
Senecio sp. (Asteraceae)	G			x		
Smilax anceps (Smilacaceae)	G	x		x		
Solanum welwitschii (Solanaceae)	G		x			
Strombosia sp. (Olacaceae)	C	x	x			
Symphonia globulifera (Guttiferaceae)	G/C	x	x			
Syzigium cordatum (Myrtacaceae)	G/C	x				
Syzigium guineense (Myrtaceae)	G/C	x	x		wood	
Teclea nobilis (Rutaceae)	G/C	x	x			
Tetrorchidium sp. (Euphorbiaceae)	G			x		
Triumphetta rhomboidea (Tiliaceae)	G			x		
Triumphetta sp. (Tiliaceae)	G/C			x		
Urera sp. (Urticaceae)	G			x	bark	
Vernonia calongensis (Compositae)	G			x	bark	
Vernonia kirungae (Compositae)	G					x
Vernonia pteropoda (Compositae)	G				bark	
Vernonia sp. (Compositae)	G/C					x
Xymalos monspora (Apocynaceae)	G/C	x	x	x		

Note: All bark/deadwood feeding records are for gorillas only; all other plant parts are shared by both species where indicated.

species group likely included *F. natalensis, F. exasperata, F. sur* (formerly *F. capensis*) and *F. vallis-choudae.*

Food Availability and Diet

Many fruits that both chimpanzees and gorillas savored were available in every month of the year during the study period. Between 23 and 57% of transect trees bore ripe fruit each month, while between 10 and 38% of trees bore new leaves each month. The number of species on which chimpanzee fed per month varied seasonally, and so did monthly fiber consumption. Gorillas' leaf-eating also varied seasonally, and the quantity of fruit they ate showed a positive correlation with the mean number of trees in fruit in the phenology transects (Spearman rank correlation N 5 12, r_s 5 .702, p < .01). The availability of fruit and the frequency with which it was consumed by chimpanzees (N 5 12, r_s 5 .189, p > .10) did not, however, show a positive correlation. At least some individuals of the trees *Ficus sp.* and *Myrianthus holstii,* the two most important chimpanzee plant foods, had ripe fruit in each month. But other food species, such as *Chrysophyllum sp.*, were highly seasonal (Nkurunungi et al. 2006). At least one fruit species, *Podocarpus milijianus*, did not fruit during the study period but fruited heavily the following year.

Unlike fruit, which often can be identified in fecal samples by its seeds, leaves and other fibrous foods are hard to identify. Ruhija chimpanzees ate much fiber in the form of THV. The gorillas' diet contained more plant species than the chimpanzees' diet did. The diet of the gorillas was 24.6% fruit; an additional 75.4% (based on Bosco's four-point abundance scale) contained leaves and herbaceous plant parts, and 21% contained bits of wood. Evidence of at least one fruit species was found in 47% of all gorilla fecal samples. The mean number of different fruit species per sample was 2.2, with a monthly range of zero to six species.

In addition to plants, we found evidence in the dung of chimpanzee meat-eating, mainly of duiker antelope (probably *Cephalophus nigrifrons*) and monkeys (probably *Cercopithecus m. mitis* and/or *C. l'hoesti*). Four percent of dung samples contained bones or skin of these mammals. About 2% of fecal samples contained remnants of safari ants (*Dorylus sp.*), and 3% contained bees or bee larvae. We observed the chimpanzees eating at least two species (*Apis mellifera* and *Meliponula brocandei*), for which they used different tools to extract the honey of each species (Stanford et al. 2000).

The gorillas ate at least two nonplant dietary items. They often ate small stones up to 0.5-meter diameter. We couldn't be sure if these were ingested incidentally while the gorillas were eating soil or were actively foraged. The stones might have been helpful with digestion, in the way that gizzard stones help some birds. Gorillas also ate wood from rotting logs, evidence of which was found in 19.4% of fecal samples.

Dietary Overlap between the Two Species

Contrary to the reputation mountain gorillas have for being foliage-eaters, in the dry seasons (February–March and May–July), Bwindi gorillas ate significantly more fruit species in their diet than chimpanzees did (Mann-Whitney U-test, U 5 5,433, p < .01). Throughout the year, gorillas and chimpanzees included similar number of plant food species in their diets (Figure 5–2; Mann-Whitney U-test, U 5 875.5, p > .05). Every chimpanzee fecal sample contained at least one fruit species, except during the months of October and December. Every gorilla fecal sample also contained at least one fruit species, except from August to December when evidence of fruit in their diet dropped to less than 10% of samples.

Gorillas and chimpanzees ate many of the same plant species. Overlap in the species of fruit eaten by the two apes showed a significant positive correlation (Spearman rank correlation, N 5 12, r_s 5 .805, p > .01). For example, when chimpanzees ate *Ficus sp.*, gorillas were also likely to be

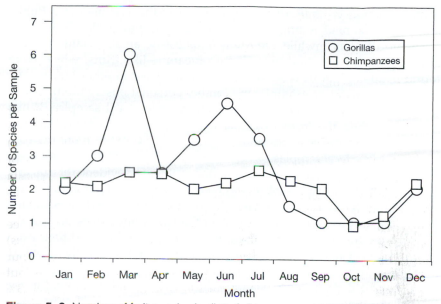

Figure 5–2 Number of fruit species in diet of chimpanzees and gorillas by month.

feeding on *Ficus sp.* (r² 5 .565, p < .01). This no doubt had to do with the cycles of fruiting; both apes homed in on ripe fruit trees.

Both apes also showed strong seasonal variation in the amount of fibrous foliage eaten. Leaves tended to be eaten more when fruit was not, in both species (gorillas; Spearman rank correlation, N 5 12, r_s 5 .607, p < .05; chimpanzees; N 5 12, r_s 5 .769, p < .001). Chimpanzees ate leafy material mainly from September to January, the same months during which fruit was least available. When fruit was readily available, chimpanzees ignored leafy foods; for example, between June and August, chimpanzees ate almost no fiber. Gorillas, on the other hand, ate a great deal of leafy foods in all months, even those in which they consumed fruit. Gorilla leaf-eating was, however, negatively correlated with the availability of fruit (Spearman rank correlation, N 5 12, r_s 5 .539, p > .05).

January and February were the peak months of fruit availability (Kruskal-Wallis test, df 5 11, U 5 121.5, p > .05), but neither chimpanzees or gorillas responded quickly to the increased supply of fruit. It was also difficult to tell how variation from year to year in fruit supply influenced ranging and foraging patterns, although it no doubt did. Although both apes fed on many of the same food species, there were differences in which species were preferred, or at least eaten most often, by each. Chimpanzees fed very heavily on *Ficus sp.*, seeds of which were in 29% of all fecal samples. Gorillas relied much less on *Ficus* (2% of gorilla fecal samples). Chimpanzees also ate fruits of *Drypetes gerrardii*, a small understory tree that is abundant in Ruhija and is also a favored nesting tree (Stanford & Nkurunungi 2003).

The gorillas, meanwhile, ate *Myrianthus holstii*, an abundant tree that grows along streams and bears large pineapple-like fruits, which were found in 20% of gorilla fecal samples. Chimpanzees in other forests love *Myrianthus* fruits (for example, in Gombe; personal observation), but in Bwindi they appeared in only 4% of chimpanzee fecal samples. While gorillas relished the fruits of *Olinia usambarensis, Maesa lanceolata,* and *Chrysophyllum gorungosanum,* none of these was present in more than 5% of chimpanzee fecal samples.

Everything I've just said needs a cautionary note. The evidence of fruit and leaf eating that I've just described was taken largely from analysis of the two species' dung, enhanced by our own observations of their feeding. Sampling the gorillas' diet was much more extensive than for chimpanzees, because the former were tracked daily and dung was found in and around their nests each morning. Chimpanzee fecal samples were collected near their feeding and nesting trees. (It's easy to distinguish chimpanzee dung from gorilla dung: Gorilla dung is enormous (at least in adults) and it is found in the immediate area of gorilla nests.)

Samples of the dung of both apes were sieved in 1-millimeter mesh sieves, and the contents were analyzed by Caleb, who was expert enough to identify most seeds and plant parts down to the species level. We checked these identifications against the reference plant collection in the Ruhija herbarium. We were able to identify many species of fruit, seeds, leaves, flowers, and also bits of bone, wood, and insects. We distinguished fiber from fruit products. We correlated the percentage of the fecal samples that were fiber versus nonfiber and compared diet with phenological data. When we were done with our analyses, we sun-dried our samples and stored them in plastic bags. Our method followed other field studies of great apes (Nishihara 1995; Remis 1997).

Our gorillas' diet was high in fruit, at least in some seasons; in some months more than half of the fecal samples contained seeds (Nkurunungi 2005). But the gorilla diet contained no fruit in other months, and then resembled the diet of gorillas in the Virungas (Watts 1984). Bwindi gorillas climbed trees far more often than Virungas gorillas, and they fed in trees on foliage, fruits, fungi, and other epiphytic plants. Even our silverback, Zeuss, climbed as high as 30 meters (almost 100 ft) above the ground, something Virungas gorillas almost never do.

The diet of the gorillas was similar to that of our chimpanzees in months when fruit was available. During the dry seasons (July–August) from 1997 to 1999, both species fed heavily on the same three fruit species: *Chrysophyllum gorungosanum, Cassina aethiopica,* and *Syzigium guineense.* But from September to December, the gorilla diet contained almost no fruit, whereas the chimpanzees continued to forage far and wide in search of fruit trees. The diet of both apes only roughly followed monthly variation in the availability of ripe fruit. Whereas fruit availability was highest in January and February, neither species responded rapidly to the increased supply of preferred food.

FALLBACK FOODS

Local people in other countries often ask me, "What is your staple food in America?" This question doesn't make much sense to us in western culture, because we eat such a variety of foods. Your weekly dinners may include pasta, burritos, sushi, curries, and stir-fry, all of which are cultural imports to the United States. But staple foods are the norm in most non-western cultures: rice in East Asia, bread in much of Europe, tortillas in Mexico, and so on. These staples are fallback foods: They are readily available, can be eaten more than once a day, and are inexpensive.

Many other animal species, including chimpanzees and gorillas, also have fallback foods. Recall that in the early days of ape research, mountain gorillas were thought to be almost exclusively folivorous, and all known chimpanzee populations were highly frugivorous. It appeared, therefore, that dietary overlap between them was minimal. This image changed as studies on lowland gorilla populations showed that they eat a diet as fruit-based as chimpanzees in the same site (Kuroda et al. 1996). Since then, researchers studying gorilla and chimpanzee ecology have focused on the availability and use of fallback foods. A fallback food is a fruit or herb that is eaten, sometimes in great quantity, not because it is the preferred food available, but rather because of its reliable availability. Such a food might be eaten only seasonally when preferred foods are not available, or may be eaten throughout the year as a staple that is easily and rapidly harvested.

Gorillas rely on THV as a fallback food (Malenky et al. 1994; Doran & McNeilage 1998), while chimpanzees apparently do not. Wrangham et al. (1993) found, however, that THV in Kibale chimpanzees' diet was negatively correlated with frugivory, suggesting that THV was a fallback food. Our analyses of chimpanzee diet were too limited to address this issue because of the difficulty of identifying herbaceous plant material. Takeshi Furuichi and his colleagues (2001) recently showed that at least one fruiting tree (*Musanga leo-errerae*) is a fallback food for chimpanzees in Kalinzu forest, Uganda. There has also been a debate over whether gorillas seek fatty fruits (Rogers et al. 1988) or avoid them (Calvert 1985), and whether chimpanzees use figs as a preferred fruit source (Janzen 1979) or a fallback food (Wrangham et al. 1993). Wrangham et al. (1991) considered figs—usually thought of as a preferred chimpanzee food—to be a readily available but relatively poor food source for Kibale chimpanzees.

Whatever figs' nutritional value is to chimpanzees, there is another important factor that predicts the occurrence of chimpanzees and gorillas in the same habitat. Gorilla populations eat less fruit in their diet at higher elevations. This is probably because fruit trees become scarce as one climbs to higher elevations. But fruit-eating by chimpanzees does not show the same pattern (Stanford & Nkurunungi 2003; Figure 5–3; r^2 5 .72, p < .01). Chimpanzees simply don't occur at very high elevations, presumably because of the absence of fruit.

There was little evidence that feeding competition occurs between Bwindi chimpanzees and gorillas. Other studies have found that chimpanzee and gorilla diets converge during times of fruit abundance, and diverge during fruit scarcity (Tutin & Fernandez 1993; Tutin 1996). The two apes have been observed to share tree crowns when fruit is scarce (Suzuki & Nishihara 1992; Yamagiwa et al. 1996). One aggressive interspecific encounter event in April 2002 (described in the next chapter) is anecdotal evidence that head-to-head competition occurs. We don't know whether direct competition is rare, or just rarely observed; future research can further address the importance of diet overlap and competition between the two species.

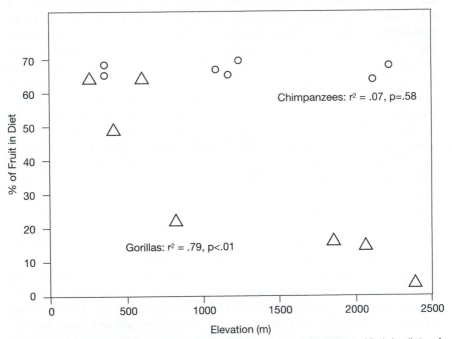

Figure 5–3 The relationship between elevation (m) and proportion of fruit in diets of chimpanzees and gorillas.
Source: Adapted from Stanford (2006a).

THE USE OF SPACE

How a wild animal uses its habitat—its *ranging* behavior—has long interested biologists. Some animals travel enormous distances each day in search of food, while others barely move at all. Among primates, even closely related species may have widely divergent travel patterns. These variations are likely linked to dietary quality, and food distribution and availability, in addition to factors such as body size (big animals tend to travel farther), and phylogenetic history. In the New World tropics, for example, howling monkeys (*Alouatta sp.*) are sedentary, moving short distances followed by long bouts of leaf-eating (Milton 1981). In the same forests, spider monkeys (*Ateles sp.*) are speedsters, scrambling through the canopy in search of ripe fruits all day long and covering several times the distances howlers travel. The study of travel patterns in nonhuman primates has progressed far in the past decade, and hypotheses are being tested that go far beyond simple correlations between diet and behavior (Boinski & Garber 2000, and papers therein).

Chimpanzee and gorilla ranging patterns have always been considered in stark contrast. Chimpanzees are highly mobile in their search for ripe fruit. Wrangham (1975) was the first to quantify this; he recorded female daily ranges of approximately 3 km/day for adult females, and more than 6 km/day (with a maximum of 10 km/day) for adult males. Male chimpanzees also travel faster than females, presumably due to the females' burden of carrying infants (Wrangham 1999). Gorillas, meanwhile, were long thought to be quite sedentary, but as we saw in Chapter 1, Caroline Tutin and others have refuted that notion.

STUDYING RANGING BEHAVIOR

There are several methods for studying the ranging behavior of primates and other animals. To study day range, one can follow the animals from dawn to dusk, recording all movements on a detailed map of the study site. Later, it's possible to measure the total distance traveled by the animals from dawn to dusk. One easy way to do this is to use a hip chain. More a thread than a chain, the researcher carries a box on his or her belt with a spool of biodegradable thread that slowly unwinds as the researcher follows the animals. This Hansel-and-Gretel method leaves an exact trail of movement throughout the day, and the spool also records total distance traveled. It is time-honored, low tech, and very useful. It is especially useful in hilly terrain, since the straight-line distance walked in mountains might be far less than is actually traversed in all the ups and downs of a daily path of travel.

Measuring annual home range—the total area of forest used by a group in the course of a year—can be done in a variety of ways. One can map the study site, then divide the site map with a grid. Each square of the grid might measure 100 × 100 meters. Each entry into each unit of the grid is recorded, and after the study period is completed, one can easily see how much time was spent in each portion of the home range, and also its overall area. This method is prone to some error, because the animals may enter small parts of each grid unit, but one records the range as though all of each grid was used. To simply estimate the size of the range, one can record all sightings of the animals, and following the end of the study period, draw a line around all those points on the map. The area of that polygon will be the estimated range size, although some areas inside the polygon that were not used will still be counted as home range. Each of these methods has a variety of pragmatic and statistical advantages and pitfalls.

Over the course of a study, the overall home range tends to increase. This is obvious in the early months of a study because the animals travel to places that they frequent, but the researcher has not observed before. But even after many months and years, primate groups will explore new areas, or return to places an older member of the group may recall as worthwhile. Consequently, a short-term study can address the size of the range only for its duration.

However, none of these methods was adequate for the kind of study we were doing in Ruhija. We were trying to identify exactly where both our chimpanzees and gorillas go, what influences those travel patterns, and how they vary by season and by year. And the critical question was how the movements of the two apes overlapped, and whether the movements of one influenced in any way the movements of the other. For this we needed more fine-scale habitat analysis. In recent years a new technology has become available to address such questions: Geographic Information Systems (GIS) using Geographic Positioning Systems (GPS) technology. We're all familiar with GPS; it's what the military devised to guide cruise missiles into enemy territory. The unit has a built-in digital map, and that map is linked to a series of orbiting satellites. The unit signals the satellite, and the signals received back tell the unit where it is. When this technology became available to the public, the precision of the instruments was intentionally limited by the military, but these days one can obtain an accurate mapping of any spot on Earth down to the nearest foot or so. This allowed us to map the study site in Ruhija in great detail. GPS readings were obtained with handheld Garmin 2[1] units, often facilitated by using 2 m remote antennas suspended overhead. One GPS recording for gorillas and one for chimpanzees was chosen per day for home range mapping and analysis. Readings were normally taken from gorilla nest sites, and from either fresh chimpanzee nests or feeding sites. Poor reception under thick vegetation or on cloudy and rainy days sometimes made it impossible to obtain GPS readings.

There is, however, one prerequisite for creating a digital map of a study site. The site must already be mapped, and that map digitized. Only after this can we use GPS units to map the locations of nests, feeding trees, and so on, and then use GIS software to plot them on the map. In the case of Bwindi, we were lucky. Because GIS has become such a powerful tool in land use and conservation, Makerere University in Kampala had a world-class GIS lab, and many Ugandan and expatriate students and staff carrying out ecological mapping and monitoring. One student project has been to digitize the existing maps of Bwindi. By carefully recording the locations of all streams, major trails, political boundaries, and forest types, the project turned a paper contour map into an interactive, highly informative digital one. We were then able to make use of the map by plotting our own GPS-collected data onto the map. This digital portrait of the landscape at Bwindi could then be analyzed by month, by year, and by any other temporal or spatial variable we chose. In this way, we produced a series of GIS maps showing the movements and locations of both gorillas and chimpanzees around the study site. Because Bosco's gorilla data collection ended in 2002, direct comparison of chimpanzees and gorillas can be made only for the period 2000–2002. During this period the Ruhija chimpanzees and gorillas shared almost exactly the same area of forest (Stanford & Nkurunungi 2003; Nkurunungi et al. 2006). Their use of the habitat, however, differed markedly, as is illustrated in the Appendix (Figures A–L). In general, months in which the chimpanzee were foraging in one area, saw the gorilla foraging in a different area of the home range.

Gorilla group movements were extensive during periods of low productivity, when their fruit intake dropped to almost zero. Although we expected that gorillas might actively move away from fruit-feeding opportunities during periods of reduced fruit abundance in response to chimpanzee party movements, we found no evidence of this. We also examined the relationship between fruit availability and proximity of the two species. For example, during 2000, while chimpanzee fruit intake was reduced for periods of approximately two months (they ate predominantly *Ficus sp.* fruits), the gorillas fed almost entirely on fibrous foods for a period of four months. The gorilla group used various vegetation types within their home range. They avoided the large swamp, dividing their range into two forest blocks. The frequency of quadrat use varied significantly among core, regularly and frequently used areas (Kruskal-Wallis test $H_{(2, N 5 34)}$ 5 27.9, p < .001). Only 7 km^2 of the total home range was used more intensively (core area) accounting for 20.6% of the total home range area (Nkurunungi et al. 2006).

The 12 smaller figures show the monthly distribution of gorilla and chimpanzee nests during 2000. Chimpanzee ranging data in July 2000 were not available. Chimpanzee and gorilla ranges showed extensive overlap, but in only two months (March and October) did nest sites overlap extensively. In other months, gorilla nests were tightly clustered in distribution, while chimpanzee nests were found in a more scattered pattern that fell entirely or almost entirely outside the range of gorilla nests.

Chimpanzee and gorilla range use was similar, but overlapped little, despite their tendency to feed on the same fruit resources (Stanford & Nkurunungi 2003). Monthly presence of chimpanzee activity was, however, generally to the east or south of gorilla activity. The Ruhija chimpanzee community ranges over roughly the same area as the Kyagurilo gorilla group, although day range length of the gorilla group (approximately 800 m) is shorter than that of most chimpanzee parties (> 1.0 km; Stanford & Nkurunungi 2003).

The total home range size measured in this study was larger than for groups in the Virungas and comparable to eastern lowland gorillas (*Gorilla g. graueri*) in Kahuzi-Biega National Park. Even within Bwindi, there were variations in home range size. These results are not surprising given that one factor that influences home range size is the availability and distribution of food resources. In Bwindi, fruit trees and food resources are patchily distributed compared to the more uniform habitat in the Virungas where preferred foods are abundant and widely distributed (Watts 1984). Virungas gorillas are strict folivores, presumably because they inhabit an area lacking in fruit tree species compared to Bwindi.

Watts (1998) and Yamagiwa et al. (1996) pointed out that even where gorilla groups and chimpanzee communities share the same area of forest, the two species exploit resources differently. Gorilla groups tend to use small parts of their home range each month, covering the entire home range only over the course of an annual cycle. Chimpanzees forage widely for fruit on a daily basis, covering large portions of their home range in a shorter time period. When important chimpanzee foods are scarce, the community disperses into small subgroups, with larger foraging parties forming mainly when ripe fruit is abundant (Goodall 1986). These divergent foraging strategies may also allow the two species to avoid feeding competition for fruit when sympatric.

6

Ruhija Discoveries

A PLACE TO SLEEP

Unlike all other primates, the great apes build sleeping nests each night. We know surprisingly little about ape nests, even though they are a major part of the evidence of their existence apes leave behind each day. A few studies (Baldwin et al. 1981; Fruth & Hohmann 1993, 1996; Sept 1998; Hernandez 2006) have used nests not only to understand patterns of great apes' behavior, but also to infer how early hominids may have used their habitats. But for the most part, despite the thousands of hours of observation of chimpanzees, what they do between dusk and dawn (other than sleep) has remained a topic of little research and little interest.

Chimpanzees carefully break branches in the crown of a tree, or in a chosen fork of limbs, and create a leafy bed. Each night of their lives, a new nest is made (although in some very arid forests nests are sometimes reused), usually high in trees. Sometimes chimpanzee also construct day nests, more flimsily and quickly made platforms for taking their midday nap. Gorillas meanwhile also make nests each night. As you might expect, gorilla nests are massive affairs, usually enormous bowls of flattened vegetation made in meadows or clearings. In Bwindi, one can easily locate a gorilla group simply by locating the nests of the previous night—easily aged by the sight of large quantities of fresh dung—and then track the animals to the current location by following their bulldozed paths through the forest undergrowth.

A part of the traditional dichotomy between gorilla and chimpanzee behavior is that chimpanzee nest only in trees but gorillas, being huge and highly terrestrial, nest on the ground. We wanted to test this dichotomy in Bwindi along with many other conventional wisdoms that seemed not to hold true for the two species. Gorilla and chimpanzee nests are very easy to tell apart (Figures 6–1 and 6–2). Gorilla nests are huge (up to 2 m across in some cases), and generally have lots of gorilla dung in and around them. Chimpanzee nests are a meter or so across, usually found in clusters where parties have slept.

Nests can provide us with an array of important behavioral and ecological information. First, since both apes make a new nest every night (at least in Bwindi), they tell us where the animals have gone. By GIS-mapping nest locations, we were able to tell with accuracy where the gorillas had been the day before, even if Bosco had not actually seen them. The choice of a sleeping nest may tell us much about habitat use. Does a chimpanzee or gorilla select a spot to make a nest because it is near a favored spot to have breakfast the next morning? Or because of certain characteristics the tree or spot might have that make it a comfortable and safe place to sleep? Perhaps the local landscape, the topography or microclimate or tree structure, influences site selection and nest-building. These were all questions we wanted to pursue when we began collecting data on chimpanzee and gorilla nests in Ruhija in January 2000.

There are many pitfalls to the interpretation of great ape behavior based on nests. For chimpanzee in particular, because of their fluid social grouping

Figure 6–1 Chimpanzees build new individual nests each night.

Figure 6–2 Gorilla nests are typically on the ground in open areas, and are massive.

pattern, nest distribution can be as confusing as it is illuminating. The presence of chimpanzee nests near the periphery of their known range could be evidence of your community, or evidence of the neighboring one. Parties sleep wherever they happen to be at nightfall, and not always clustered closely together, so an aggregation of nests may or may not indicate the size of the party.

The major uncertainty about the nests of either gorillas or chimpanzees is aging them. A freshly made nest is still composed of green, fresh-looking leaves a day or two later. But within a few days the leaves wither on the branches broken in making the nest, and the nest takes on a shriveled appearance. This continues until the nest, weeks to months later, is just a tangle of dead leaves and dry twigs. Although some researchers have felt they could determine the age of a nest in the forest with some accuracy (Ghiglieri 1984), most (e.g., Plumptre & Reynolds 1997) have felt nests cannot be reliably aged. The vagaries of rainfall, humidity, and characteristics of the nest tree species all confound dating the nest of either ape species.

We got around this problem by recording the discovery of all fresh nests. Beginning in January 2000, data on all nests found in the study site by field assistants were recorded. These data included tree and nest height, tree species, elevation, and the proximity of other nests. After this we only collected information about new nests that were located. We categorized nests as *fresh* (1–2 days old, full of fresh green leaves), *new* (not fresh but still green), *old* (withered leaves), and *very old* (from very dry and dead to falling apart).

Although most gorilla nests were found on the ground as in the mountain gorilla populations in the Virungas, about 24% were made in trees. Jessica Rothman and colleagues (2006) found that Bwindi gorillas preferred to make ground nests in bracken ferns (*Pteridium sp.*). When made in trees, their nests were almost always in the same tree species, *Alchornea floribunda*, a small spreading understory tree. Given the massive size of a gorilla nest, such a tree geometry may have been necessary for support. The other 76% of nests were typical mountain gorilla nests, enormous bowls usually flattened in meadows of bracken ferns. The size of the nest indicated the size of the maker, and the additional presence of dung often indicated whether the occupant had been the silverback male or one of the females.

Chimpanzee nests were made in trees 94% of the time. Nests were found at all the elevations of the study site. The height ranged in accordance with the height of the nesting tree. However, unlike other east African chimpanzee populations that have been studied, Bwindi chimpanzees sometimes nested on the ground. About 6% of all chimpanzee nests were found on the ground. Although we couldn't be positive whether they were night nests or day nests, their construction was similar to that of night nests: branches broken over firmly to form a bowl-shaped bed. The notable difference was that sapling trees were broken over a meter above the ground, instead of branches high in tree canopies. There was also an unusual uniformity to the ways the nests were situated. Ground nests were always found on steep hillsides (not unexpected given the prevalence of steep slopes in Bwindi), lying on top of fallen tree trunks. The nests were oriented so that a fallen log would support the downhill side of the nest, with the uphill side lying against the steep ground. The effect was a flat leafy mattress.

Chimpanzee ground nests were much more common outside the study area, in the Kayonza section of the park. This is the smaller, triangular piece of Bwindi that is nearly cut off from the main lower section by a stretch of cultivated land. Kayonza is the lowest elevation part of the park, averaging approximately 900–1,200 meters. Why chimpanzee ground nests would be more common here was unclear. A possibility that initially seemed the likely major factor in ground nesting was the absence of leopard. Leopard are believed to be locally extinct, or at least extremely rare in Bwindi; there have been no confirmed reports in or around the park for many years. Without their major predators (lion have been gone from Bwindi for many years also), chimpanzees would have little to fear while sleeping on the ground, especially in elephant-free areas. However, a student volunteering on the project for a summer, Johanna Maughn, discovered an old account of a wildlife survey in Bwindi in the 1950s that reported *both* the presence of leopard and the occurrence of chimpanzee ground nests (Albrecht & Dunnett 1971). This casts doubt on any straightforward ecological explanation for ground nesting.

Two other factors that might be related to the presence of ground nests in this part of the park but no other are the absence of both elephants and gorillas. A herd of approximately 30 elephants lives in Bwindi, spending nearly all their time in the larger southern block of the park. Without the danger of elephants wandering around at night, chimpanzee might be more likely to forgo night nesting. The park's gorillas also do not occur in the low-lying Kayonza forest. If nest site competition is a factor at all in tree nesting (unlikely with a population density of 1.0 km^2 for each species), chimpanzee might more readily nest on the ground in areas without gorillas. Given that Bwindi is wet and chilly at night, and the ground especially so, it doesn't seem likely that ground nesting would have been perpetuated through the decades if it were purely a local cultural tradition. But we cannot refute this possibility.

Choosing a Place to Sleep

The choice of nesting sites has been of surprisingly little interest to field primatologists over the years. Furuichi and Hashimoto (2004) recently examined how landscape and vegetation influence nest site selection, but the choice of particular places to nest, and even whether selectivity is occurring, has been little studied. We analyzed the choice of nesting sites for 3,414 nests located between 2000 and 2004 (Table 6–1). There are more than 160 tree species in Bwindi Impenetrable National Park (Butynski 1984), of

Table 6–1 Choice of Sleeping Trees by Ruhija Chimpanzees, 2000–2004

	2000	*2001*	*2002*	*2003*	*2004*
Cassipourea sp.	10.9%	17.7%	15.0%	11.9%	13.3%
Chrysophyllum sp.	22.3%	16.9%	13.1%	17.4%	14.6%
Drypetes sp.	17.5%	19.5%	29.5%	26.0%	23.1%
Teclea nobilis	17.3%	19.9%	25.3%	26.0%	18.9%

which at least 38 were used for nest-building by the Ruhija chimpanzees during the five year period. *Parinari sp., Chrysophyllum sp.,* and *Newtonia sp.* dominate many regions of the park (Howard 1991; Bitariho 1999) but only *Chrysophyllum sp.* were preferred nesting trees for the Ruhija chimpanzees. Four tree species (*Cassipourea sp., Chrysophyllum sp., Drypetes sp.,* and *Teclea nobilis*) accounted for approximately 72% of all nests.

Most nests (93%) were constructed in food tree species, though we could not determine from our data whether those trees were actively fruiting at the time of nesting. The use of food tree species was certainly not proportional to their overall availability. The chimpanzees were feeding in *Ficus sp.* during 82% of feeding scan samples of parties observed from 2000–2004, but fewer than 2% of all nests were constructed in *Ficus sp.* during this period. There was no consistent correlation from month to month between the use of trees for feeding and use of trees for nests for *Ficus sp.* or for the four preferred nesting tree species (Stanford & O'Malley Unpublished data).

Using tree abundance data for 11 tree species from Nkurunungi (2005), 10 species were used as nests by the Ruhija chimpanzees. A Spearman's rank correlation found no significant relationship between the density of these tree species in the study area and the number of nests constructed in each tree species during the study period (r_s 5 .241, n 5 11, p 5 .474).

We conducted additional analyses on the 15 most commonly used tree species (each with a nest count of n $ 30) which together accounted for 93% of all nests. A series of pair-wise Wilcoxon signed ranks tests found no significant differences in relative tree species preferences between any of the five years of the study (Stanford & O'Malley Unpublished data).

In other words, the Ruhija chimpanzees used a subset of trees in the study site for nesting, and tended to select food tree species for nesting. We can't say, however, that they actively chose their nesting trees, as opposed to simply stopping for the night wherever their travels that day had taken them.

From 2000 through 2004, the work at Ruhija continued uninterrupted; my field trips to the site continued, though they became less frequent after 2003. But the field assistants did a wonderful job cataloging chimpanzee and gorilla behavior, and slowly breaking down the shyness of the chimpanzees so we could learn more about them. Most of the day-to-day data we collected were fairly prosaic: the percentage of leaves and fruit in the diet; the percentage of time the apes spent resting, moving, or feeding; and so on. Gorillas spend only a relatively small amount of time socializing in a given day. Many observers of both chimpanzees and gorillas have noted that it would take a month to see as much gorilla sex and violence as chimpanzees engage in every day. But because of our interest in how the ecologies of the two species were alike and different, every data point was interesting and important. There was the central issue of compilation of monthly, seasonal, and annual changes in plant availability in relation to chimpanzee and gorilla diet (Chapter 5). But new observations by Bosco emerged; he reported that the gorillas ingested stones, which then turned up in their feces (Nkurunungi 2005). Whether these were ingested on purpose, as gizzard stones to aid in digestion, or incidentally along with plants foods, is unknown. The gorillas also consumed rotting wood, which they clearly sought out and relished; they would sit around fallen tree trunks and gnaw eagerly at the spots where the decomposing wood was soft. We didn't know whether there was a particular nutrient or mineral they were after in the wood, or if perhaps they were seeking fungi, which grows in rotting wood, or simply enjoying the taste.

BIPEDAL CHIMPANZEES?

In May 2001 I was at Bwindi when the field assistants reported that a large fig tree was laden with ripe fruit near the Kajembejembe trail, and the whole community was feeding in it. For the next ten days, Gervase, Bosco, and I set off at dawn in hopes of getting closer to the chimpanzees than we had previously. We spent several wonderful days sitting on the lush green mountainside, watching the chimps in a huge *Ficus natalensis* across a small ravine. When in fruit, these huge figs provide a week-long banquet for chimpanzees, and this one was no exception. The fig's uppermost branches were partially bare, and rose above the rest of the forest, so we also had a perfect eye-level view of the chimpanzees and their behavior. This allowed us to sort out things like dominance: who displaced whom at feeding spots, and who gave submissive pant grunts to whom. We learned that week that Mboneire was the clear alpha male, and that the more obsequious Kushoto was his ally, based on the pattern of pant grunts we observed.

But that wasn't all we learned. That first morning, as we watched the chimpanzees, an adult female, Martha, fed on handfuls of ripe figs, her daughter May by her side. She reached up and deftly plucked the fruits, popping them in her mouth. As we watched, she casually raised her body upright and stood on the branch, grasping a supporting limb with her left hand while she continued to feed with the other. This was not so unusual—many animals, including many primate species—stand erect for brief periods. After a few seconds Martha dropped back onto all fours. Then she moved along the branch a few steps, and stoop up *again*. And again, and again. And then we watched as Mboneire approached the spot where Martha fed and also stood up to pluck fruit. At this point I pulled out my notebook and began recording and timing the frequency and the duration of their standing up. I continued this all day; on average someone in the foraging party was standing upright about once every twenty minutes that first day. Throughout the ten days the chimpanzee stayed in that huge fig tree, they stood on their hind legs periodically, always while feeding. Males did it somewhat more often than females, and adults did it far more often than juveniles or infants. I thought back to my days watching chimpanzees at Gombe in Tanzania. Gombe chimpanzees are the most watched wild apes on Earth, but I could not remember anyone commenting on them standing up as often as these Ruhija chimpanzees.

Why was I so intrigued by this behavior? The how and why of earliest human bipedalism is one of the most hotly debated topics in science. Most scholars in earlier generations believed that the earliest hominids became bipedal (upright walking and standing) because they evolved from a quadrupedal ape that had moved out of the forest and onto the grassland in East Africa. For some unknown reason, these ancestors began to stand and travel upright for brief periods. Some have argued that these first bipeds evolved from knuckle-walking, chimpanzee-like apes whose descendants became efficient open-country walkers (Washburn 1968; Johanson et al. 1982; Lovejoy 1988). Others have posited that the early bipeds walked upright but also relied on a retained climbing adaptation (Jungers 1982; Stern & Susman 1983). Still others believe some adaptations to tree-living, such as vertical climbing (Prost 1980; Fleagle et al. 1981; Gebo 1986) or arm-swinging (Keith 1923), must have been the precursors to terrestrial bipedalism.

Of course, fossil discoveries are the key to clarifying these issues, and some recent fossil finds have helped (Leakey et al. 2001; Pickford & Senut 2001; Brunet et al. 2002). But these discoveries have not answered the question, why did our ancestors become bipeds? We know that the earliest precursors to bipeds must have had good reasons to stand up, with enhanced reproductive success for doing so. But we still do not know why the transition to bipedalism happened. Field observations of what great apes do is one key piece in the puzzle. Theories to account for standing upright range from energetic efficiency (Rodman & McHenry 1980, Leonard & Robertson 1997; Steudel 1994) to terrestrial feeding advantages (Jolly 1970), food-carrying (Lovejoy 1981), social displays (Jablonski & Chaplin 1993), and even thermoregulation (Wheeler 1984; Falk 1990). Each of these theories is compelling in its way, and each has serious flaws.

In some insightful papers, my colleague Kevin Hunt of Indiana University pointed out (1994, 1996) that the advent of bipedalism probably involved behaviors in which the ape/hominids frequently engaged. Russell Tuttle (1975, 1981), and Michael Rose (1984) had argued that bipedalism arose from the energetic advantages gained by an ape that occasionally moved bipedally between arboreal feeding sites. Hunt (1994, 1998) extended the foraging hypothesis based on his observations of arboreal bipedal small-fruit feeding by free-ranging chimpanzees in Gombe and Mahale National Parks, Tanzania. He reported two postures associated with bipedalism. First, his chimpanzees stood on arboreal substrates while plucking small fruits from overhead, often assisted by one-armed support. They also stood bipedally on the forest floor while reaching up to pull down low-hanging, fruit-laden branches. In both cases the wild chimpanzees used bipedal posture to enhance their access to fruits. Hunt's findings supported a strong arboreal component to the behavioral repertoire of both the last common ancestor and the earliest hominids.

In the only other field study of chimpanzee bipedal behavior, Diane Doran (1993) reported fifteen instances of bipedalism in a seven-month study in Taï National Park, Ivory Coast. Seven of these instances occurred in trees, all in the context of feeding. Doran did not note whether the study subjects were foraging for leaves or fruit while standing bipedally.

Although chimpanzees don't stand upright very often, the context for this behavior is of great interest to human evolutionary scientists. Hunt (1998) found that chimpanzees rarely engaged in bipedal posture (0.17 times per hour of observation), and that most of these bipedal events occurred in the context of foraging. Branch diameters were estimated to the nearest centimeter visually through binoculars, and tree heights and crown diameters were estimated to the nearest meter using range finders and (for crown diameters) straight-line measurement made on the ground. Bipedal posture and locomotion were recorded in the course of sampling a range of behavioral data; other positional behavior variables were not recorded. Bipedalism occurred as part of a complex and fluid set of behaviors. Bipedalism was recorded whenever a chimpanzee stood with most of its weight supported by its legs for at least five seconds; the five-second criteria was chosen because it meant the animal held the position for at least three seconds after rising onto its legs. Following Hunt (1998), this bipedal posture by Bwindi chimpanzees was called "unassisted bipedalism." If the chimpanzee used one or both arms to support itself on branches, but most of its body weight still appeared to be supported by its legs, it was considered to be engaging in "assisted bipedalism." The latter occurred most often, and described the positional behavior of Bwindi chimpanzees when they were engaged in arboreal bipedal feeding.

Bwindi Bipedalism

We observed 179 instances of bipedalism of five seconds or more, among 13 individuals covering 247 observation hours. This rate, 0.79 bouts/hour, was higher than reported in any other study (Table 6–2). The mean duration of bipedal bouts was twelve seconds, with a range from five seconds (the minimum duration for which an event was recorded) to 66 seconds. Most instances of standing upright were brief: 110 of 179 bouts (61.4%) lasted only five to eight seconds and only two bouts lasted more than one minute.

We saw bipedalism only in trees, on branches more than 5 meters above the ground, and usually higher. Although I suspected the chimpanzees

Table 6–2 Comparison of Bwindi Chimpanzee Bipedal Bouts with Those Recorded by Hunt (1994, 1998) in Mahale

Site	Observation hours (N)	Bipedal Bouts/hour	% Postural
Bwindi	246.7	0.73	99.4
Mahale	571	0.17	84.8

Source: Adapted from Stanford (2006b).

were sometimes bipedal on the ground, too, observation conditions at Bwindi were so poor because of dense undergrowth that we would have been very unlikely to observe it. We did not see the shuffling bipedalism that others (Hunt 1994) have reported for chimpanzees, which some researchers (Wrangham 1980) have believed to be used by early bipeds. The only bipedal walking we saw was by one female who took several bipedal steps on a large branch, assisted by arm support.

The Ruhija chimps employed bipedal posture in a variety of positions that shifted frequently and fluidly between bipedalism and quadrupedalism. While feeding, a chimpanzee would stand upright plucking fruits overhead, and while reaching for another branch, it might slowly ease into one-legged assisted bipedalism. As the animal's body moved forward toward the sought-after branch, the arms took on the majority of body support and the chimpanzee moved into an arm-hanging posture, or brachiated to the next tree limb. The chimpanzees shifted smoothly among unassisted bipedal, assisted bipedal, and quadrupedal climbing and standing postures. Arm-hanging and arm-aided support were a key component of bipedal feeding. At least one arm helped to support the animal during some portion of a bipedal bout in 169 of 179 (94.4%) instances of observed bipedalism.

Every instance of bipedalism occurred while chimpanzees were in large trees. Only one instance was locomotor bipedalism; all the others occurred while feeding (Table 6–3). All bipedal bouts were observed in one of only three tree species: *Ficus sp.* (probably *F. natalensis*), *Chrysophyllum sp.* (probably *C. gorungosanum*), and *Olea capensis*. The distribution of large *Ficus sp.* is patchy and few individuals are in fruit at the same time (Nkurunungi 2005). *Chrysophyllum sp.* and *Olea capensis* are abundant trees that grows in stands. The chimpanzees were more frequently bipedal in *Ficus sp.* than in the other two species (t 5 5.85, df 5 3, p < .01).

Ficus and *Chrysophyllum* are very large trees, reaching heights of more than 40 meters. We did not try to measure the distribution or abundance of fruit in the trees' crowns. Chimpanzees foraged bipedally most often when feeding in the upper portions of the crowns, reaching up to branches emergent in the sunlight, and perhaps containing harder-to-reach ripe fruit. When *Ficus* crops ripened, chimpanzee parties moved into the crowns to feed and remained there all day long until the fruit was visibly depleted,

Table 6–3 Summary of the Context of Bipedalism for Different Age–Sex Classes

	Feed	Stand	Walk	Total
AM	81	2	0	83
AF	64	5	1	70
JUV	25	0	0	25
INF	1	0	0	1
TOTAL	171	7	1	179

AM5 Adult male; AF5 Adult female; JUV5 juvenile; INF5 infant (see text for definitions of age–sex classes).

Source: Adapted from Stanford (2006b).

sometimes nesting nearby and returning to the same large tree the next day. We made most of our observations of bipedalism while foraging parties fed on such large fruit crops. *Ficus* and *Chrysophyllum* possess large limbs with diameters up to 50 centimeter that serve as broad substrates on which chimpanzees stand while plucking fruits from the next branch overhead. We also saw bipedal feeding on smaller branches, such as when the chimps were feeding in *Olea capensis*.

Branch size influenced both the frequency and duration of bipedalism. The frequency of feeding upright showed a significant positive correlation with branch diameter (Figure 6–3; r^2 5 .691, p < .001). Bipedal bout duration showed a weaker but significant positive correlation with branch diameter (Figure 6–4; r^2 5 .275, p < .05). Bipedalism occurred only on branches over 10 centimeter diameter, and most bipedal bouts occurred on branches over 15 centimeter diameter. Smaller branches were visibly bent and shaken by the weight of adult chimpanzees standing briefly on them.

In Hunt's earlier study, the size of the fruit consumed was an important influence on bipedal foraging. He reported that small fruit selection was positively correlated with bipedal posture, from forest floor foraging sites. Fruit size at Bwindi, however, was not correlated with either bipedal bout frequency or duration.

Although adult male chimpanzees didnot forage upright more often than other age-sex classes, their bipedal bouts were significantly longer (t 5 6.77, df 5 3, p < .05). Males and females of all ages stood up at least occasionally, although we only once saw an infant (individuals estimated under five years of age) forage this way. I observed 25 bipedal bouts by juveniles (individuals of estimated age 5 to 14 years), comprising only three individuals. On three occasions females stood and fed bipedally with infants clinging to their backs. Although there appeared to be some degree of social facilitation of bipedal foraging, there was no evidence that nearest neighbor proximity was significantly correlated with either bipedal bout frequency (r^2 5 0.011, p 5 .15) or bout duration (r^2 5 .018, p 5 .11).

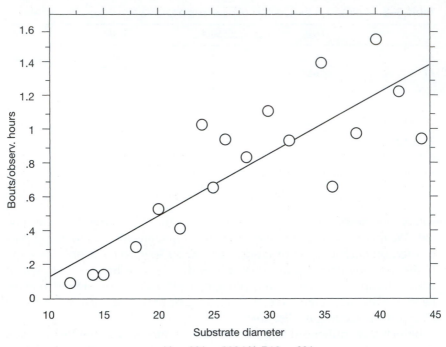

Y= −.221 + .036 * X; R^2 = .691

Figure 6–3 Relationship between substrate diameter and frequency of bipedalism by bwindi chimpanzees.
Source: Adapted from Stanford (2006b).

WHY SO BIPEDAL?

Why are the Ruhija chimpanzees so bipedal? One possibility is that they are actually not more bipedal than chimpanzees elsewhere. Instead, it may be that Bwindi's rugged terrain simply offered an ideal setting in which to observe the full range of chimpanzee upright posture. Researchers usually observe chimpanzees from the ground, far beneath their study subjects. But Bwindi's many steep-sided ravines—on which large fruit trees often grow— means that most observations of arboreal bipedalism were made at eye level. In such a setting it is much easier to notice and observe vertical changes in posture. There is also less foliage obstructing one's view. It's entirely possible that chimpanzees at other sites are also more bipedal than has been appreciated, but field conditions have prevented researchers from readily observing it. However, some sites where chimpanzees have been studied are almost as hilly as Bwindi, such as Gombe National Park in Tanzania. Other than Hunt's (1998) work there, little mention has been made in published literature of arboreal bipedal behavior at Gombe.

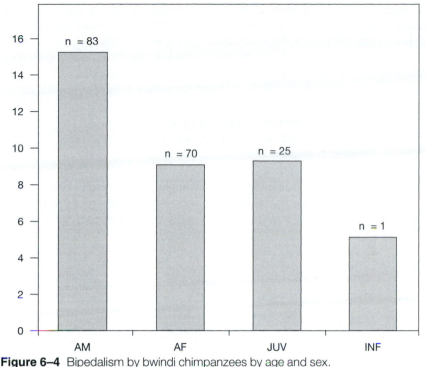

Figure 6–4 Bipedalism by bwindi chimpanzees by age and sex.
Source: Adapted from Stanford (2006b).

If the Ruhija chimpanzees truly are more bipedal than chimpanzees elsewhere, there are several possible explanations. First, the forest at Bwindi may contain more branches on which bipedalism is possible than other chimpanzee study sites. This might be due to the steep terrain or the composition of tree species. We have found little evidence of this, but detailed vegetation comparisons with other forest tracts are still in progress (Nkurunungi 2005; Nkurunungi et al. 2004). After my first observations of arboreal bipedalism at Bwindi, in large *Ficus* trees growing at steep angles from steep ravine slopes, I hypothesized that the frequency of bipedalism among the Ruhija chimpanzee community was due to an unusual number of large-diameter, parallel horizontal substrates on which feeding chimpanzees could stand upright (Stanford 2002). Further observations in the same forest, however, suggested no such bias toward odd-angled trees.

Second, chimpanzees might forage bipedally if they possessed injuries or disabilities to the upper body, such as snare wounds or amputations. In the 1960s, an outbreak of the crippling disease polio left one adult male (Faben) without the use of his arm, and he began to walk bipedally (Bauer 1977; Goodall 1986). Wounds and amputations caused by snares are common among chimpanzees in some African forests: In Budongo Forest Reserve in Uganda more than one-third of all adults are missing at least one hand or foot as a result (Waller & Reynolds 2001; Quiatt et al. 2002).

However, snare wounds are thankfully rare in the Ruhija chimpanzees. This may be the result of the low number of snares (compared to other chimpanzee study sites) that have been found by rangers patrolling the forest. Only two individuals possessed a snare wound, making it unlikely that snares have any effect on Ruhija chimp bipedal posture.

A third possibility is that Ruhija chimpanzee bipedalism may be a cultural tradition. Learned traditions are widespread in great ape behavior and are not necessarily ecologically adaptive (Whiten et al. 1999). Standing upright while foraging may not be adaptive or ecologically more efficient (in terms of fruit-harvesting rate) than other modes of feeding. If arboreal bipedalism is a cultural behavior, we should see it in young chimpanzees whose mothers stand upright more often than those whose mothers do not. Of 26 instances of bipedalism by juvenile or infant chimpanzees, 14 were by chimpanzees whose mothers also foraged bipedally. So while it is difficult to prove a behavior has a cultural basis or influence, this remains a possibility.

Despite these possible explanations for why Ruhija chimpanzees forage upright, none is so persuasive that we can rule out the starting proposition: Poor conditions for observing arboreal bipedalism at other chimpanzee study sites may have yielded observational bias at those sites. If observation condition differences explain the high incidence of Bwindi bipedalism, then observers should note bipedalism at other hilly sites, such as Gombe, as well. Although it appears that bipedalism occurs at an unusually high frequency at Bwindi, it may be that other researchers simply have not noted upright foraging in their own sites.

CLOSE ENCOUNTERS

One morning during 2001, Bosco and I sat in a hillside fern meadow about 50 meters from the Ruhija chimpanzees. The chimps were feeding in a fig tree: Mboneire, Martha, and May fed side by side. Kushoto popped figs into his mouth with his crippled hand, and other chimpanzees could be heard even at this distance moving about the lower canopy looking for food. As we watched the action, a huge dark head appeared in my binocular's field of view. My first reaction was that an enormous new chimpanzee had arrived to join the fig feeding frenzy. "Who's that big guy ?" I asked Bosco. "It's not someone we've seen before." Judging from the size of the top of his head, the new arrival must be the biggest chimpanzee I've seen in this forest.

Looking through his binoculars, Bosco answered in a quietly dramatic voice, "That's not a chimpanzee. It's a gorilla!" It was indeed a gorilla, an adult female who was slowly and cautiously climbing up into the crown of the *Ficus*, feeding as she moved. Double the size of the male chimpanzees, the female gorilla approached to within just a few meters of them, and both ape species fed on the same large tree limb. Although they must have been vividly aware of each other, both the chimpanzee party and the gorilla acted completely oblivious to the other's presence. We watched the scene for a half-hour, until the gorilla caught sight of us and fled to the ground below. She was not from the Kyagurilo research group; whether she was in the company of other gorillas was unknown but highly likely. Bosco believed she was a member of the unhabituated and shy Ruhija gorilla group.

Seeing two great ape species together in the wild is only possible in the equatorial belt of African forests inhabited by both chimpanzees and gorillas. Bonobos do not occur sympatrically with either of their kin (some scholars have suggested that the bonobo's isolation has led to some of its ecological traits). Orangutans occur sympatrically with gibbons in Indonesia, which are lesser apes, but no other great ape occurs in Asia. In Africa, chimpanzees and lowland gorillas (*Gorilla gorilla gorilla, G.g. diehlii,* and *G.b. graueri*) occur in broad sympatry across a wide area, but are known to occur together only in the lowland rain forests of central Africa, from Gabon in the west to eastern Democratic Republic of Congo in the east. And as we have seen, chimpanzees also occur sympatrically with one population of mountain gorillas in one small patch of forest in Uganda, which is Bwindi. Researchers in several sites—Lopé in Gabon (Tutin & Fernandez 1985), Ndoki in the Congo and in the Central African Republic (Kuroda et al. 1996), Kahuzi-Biega in D.R.C. (Basabose & Yamagiwa 1997), and recently Goualougo in the Republic of Congo (Morgan & Sanz, in press)—have reported chimpanzees and lowland gorillas feeding together. None of these observations occurred frequently enough to draw any conclusions about the ecological relationship between chimpanzees and gorillas. Because my study in Bwindi was conceived of as a way to infer aspects of the sympatric ecology of early hominids, observing the two apes together was intended as a key part of the study. It seemed clear that our brief observation of chimps and the gorillas together in 2001 was something few scientists had previously witnessed, but might be a hint of many more such observations to come.

The apes, however, did not cooperate. During the years we worked in Nkuringo, we had a few suggestions of actual contact between chimpanzees and gorillas, just enough to tease us that something more was happening. One day, as Mitch Keiver, Gervase, and I hiked around Nkuringo, we heard the roar of a gorilla coming from about 100–200 meters away. A split second later, a chorus of chimpanzee pant hoots erupted from what seemed to be the same place. By the time we arrived at the area the apes had left, but we all agreed the most likely explanation was that a silverback had wandered into a party of chimpanzees, to the displeasure of both sides. Michele Goldsmith also found evidence in Nkuringo of chimpanzees and gorillas having built nests on the same night in adjacent trees. And the field assistants and rangers described seeing both apes in the same place at the same time on a number of occasions, in both Nkuringo and Ruhija.

That first good observation of an encounter in 2001 was, therefore, both a reward and a disappointment. After years watching the animals, why hadn't we seen this happen more often? We had one habituated gorilla group, and as far as we knew, they had not encountered chimpanzee at close range at all until this day. The chimpanzees, being shy, could not be followed closely and we could not be certain about their whereabouts many days. The home ranges of the gorilla group and the chimpanzee community overlapped almost completely. It appeared that they either avoided each other, or else we had incredibly bad luck.

The field assistants witnessed encounters such as the one described above three more times in the following months. Then, in April 2002, we recorded our first prolonged chimpanzee–gorilla encounter in which the two species were most certainly not oblivious to one another. The field assistants that day were sitting quietly in the undergrowth, watching a party of nine chimpanzees, including two adult males, feeding in the crown of a huge *Chrysophyllum gorungosanum* tree. Midway through the morning, a group of gorillas—the habituated Kyagurilo group, as it turned out—approached and began to feed on fallen fruits on the forest floor under the same tree. Because previously observed encounters had involved either unhabituated, shy gorillas, or unhabituated chimpanzees, this was the very first opportunity in many years to see what happened when the two ape species met.

The field assistants listened to the sounds of the gorillas, hidden in dense undergrowth, munching fallen fruits for more than an hour. Then Mutu began to climb the trunk of the *Chrysophyllum*. The tree was almost 50 meters tall, and had a large fork about 10 meters up. Mutu ascended slowly to the fork, while other gorillas on the ground appeared to be preparing to climb into the *Chrysophyllum* also. But at that moment, several of the chimpanzees, including the two males, stopped feeding and raced down the tree to the fork, screaming at the gorillas. Mutu stopped, and other gorillas that had just begun to climb the trunk stopped in their tracks also. What followed was an hour of chimpanzee bravado; the two males, Kushoto and Kidevu, repeat-edly slapped branches with their hands and gave screams that seemed both aggressive and fearful to the observers. The impasse was finally broken when a group of park rangers happened by the place in search of the gorillas. Their noise startled the chimpanzees, who fled the scene. As soon as the chimpanzees left, the gorillas calmly climbed into the tree crown and began to feed on the *Chrysophyllum* fruits.

What do we make of this encounter? It certainly seemed as though the chimpanzees, though outnumbered by the much larger gorillas, were able to hold their larger cousins at bay while they themselves fed in the treetops. In doing so, they granted themselves unlimited access to the *Chrysophyllum* fruits, latexlike large fruits (in the family Sapotaceae) that are one of the favored plant foods of both chimpanzees and gorilla in Ruhija. It is interesting that in the other four encounters between chimps and gorillas, there was no aggression at all, and all these encounters occurred in *Ficus* trees. *Ficus* are a major food for chimps, although researchers have differed as to whether they are a preferred food or simply a less preferred but reliable fallback (Wrangham et al. 1993). Although the number of observations is small, it's intriguing that in all five observed encounters, gorillas arrived late on the scene and tried to feed in the same tree in which chimps were already feeding. But only in the *Chrysophyllum* tree did the chimpanzees respond aggressively or competitively. This suggests that *Chrysophyllum* may be a more valued food source than *Ficus,* one worth defending.

There has been some research on the nature of ecological competition between chimpanzees and the other primates with which they share a habitat. Alain Houle and colleagues (in press) found that in Kibale National Park, Uganda, chimpanzees occupied a position of ecological dominance relative to the several species of monkey with which they often share the crowns of fruiting trees. When chimpanzees and red-tailed monkeys (*Cercopithecus ascanius*) blue monkeys (*Cercopithecus mitis*), or grey-cheeked mangabeys (*Lophocebus albigena*) fed in the same tree, chimpanzees occupied the prime feeding spots, ate the most fruit, and also wasted the most uneaten, dropped fruit. The fruit growing in the upper parts of the tree crown tended to ripen earlier and to reach larger sizes. The density of fruits was higher in the upper crown, and their sugar content was higher (Houle 2004). These differences were probably related to the greater availability of sunlight on the upper branches.

The monkeys, meanwhile, fed lower in the tree and therefore on less desirable patches of food. However, they also found that the monkeys foraged more efficiently. They discarded less uneaten fruit, and consumed more fruits per unit of time spent foraging. To Houle, it appeared that the chimpanzees, having controlled the food patch, could afford to be wasteful, whereas the monkeys could not. The dominance of chimpanzees was apparently related to their large size, as there was a linear dominance hierarchy among the five primate species based on body weight.

Chimpanzees display, therefore, clear ecological dominance in a feeding context over sympatric monkeys. In Bwindi, however, they also appear to be dominant over the much larger-bodied gorillas. The explanation for this, albeit based on only a few observations, may be related to behavioral differences between the two apes. Chimpanzees display a far higher rate of intragroup agonistic social interaction than gorillas do (Goodall 1986). This greater willingness to resort to aggression may lead chimpanzees to respond aggressively to gorillas before the latter would be likely to respond aggressively to them.

7

Hominid Coexistence?

To try to understand the likely relationship between two similar species sharing a habitat, we turn to ecological theory. The principle of competitive exclusions is at the heart of the study of sympatric species. It states that two species cannot share the same habitat if they have identical needs for the same resources. Crawley (1986) describes competition as those interactions between two species that contribute to an increase in one species' population density and simultaneously to a decrease in the population density of the other species. The idea is drawn originally from early mathematical models of interspecies competition of the mathematicians Lotka and Volterra. Demonstrating the exclusionary effects of competition has proved to be far more difficult in nature than in a laboratory or mathematical equation, however. The complexity of natural ecosystems provides numerous confounding factors, such as predation, and the uncertainty of whether food resources are truly limiting, that make it difficult to tease apart the effects of head-to-head competition. At one time, ecologists believed that interspecies competition was the force that provided most of the order and pattern in forest communities (Cody & Diamond 1975). Other schools of ecological thinking have, however, strongly disagreed that ecological communities are so tightly ordered or that competition is such an important force (Strong et al. 1984). Because of the difficulties inherent in demonstrating that competition is a strong evolutionary force, researchers usually talk in terms of niche separation and niche overlap rather than assume such divergences are the result of head-to-head competition.

It is clear, nonetheless, that two closely related species living in the same habitat typically diverge in some key aspects of their behavior, ecology, or anatomy. Lions and leopards live together across much of Africa, but lions hunt big game in open country, whereas leopards spend more time in thickets, hunting game of all sizes. Diet is often the main point of divergence. We can infer the results of ecological competition in the fossil record, because diet is often reflected in the anatomy of the teeth, which are often well preserved in long-extinct fossil specimens. For instance, among Olduvai's early human species there was one, *Homo habilis,* that possessed small, unimpressive molar teeth and a generally modestly proportioned skull. Another, *Australopithecus boisei,* was the owner of massive molars and a skull that featured a bony crest down the midline. These features indicate *A. boisei's* adaptation to a diet of tough, fibrous, or hard-shelled foods. Fossil researchers believe this dietary difference allowed these two human ancestors to survive in the same place without lethal competition between them for many millennia. These sorts of ecological niche divergences are widespread in nature—they allow multiple species, including closely related ones, to share the same habitat, and are a driving force behind the formation of new species.

So what can information about chimpanzees and gorillas in Bwindi tell us about the lives of these early hominids? We hope to use such field data on sympatric African apes, in combination with the fossil record and ecological principles, to tease out some answers to human evolutionary questions. Assuming that extinct species obeyed the same evolutionary principles that living ones do, we can make well-informed guesses about grouping patterns, foraging behavior and diet, range use, nesting pattern, and tool use.

Between one and five million years ago, there were several times and places when more than one hominid taxon occupied the same geographic area. At least four different early hominid forms lived in close proximity or sympatry between 2.5 and 3.0 million years ago (Table 7–1). *Homo habilis* (some researchers would call *H. habilis* by another name, *H. rudolfensis*), and *Australopithecus boisei* coexisted at Olduvai Gorge between 1.5 and 1.9 million years ago (Leakey 1959, 1966). *H. erectus* (early forms of which are sometimes

Table 7–1 Possible Cases of Sympatry among Pliocene Hominids Based on Current Fossil Evidence

Date	Location	Species	Species	Species
3.5 mya	East Africa	*Australopithecus afarensis*	*Kenyanthropus platyops*	
2.5 mya	East Africa	*Australopithecus garhi*	*Australopithecus aethiopicus*	*Early Homo*
2.0–2.3 mya	East Africa	*Australopithecus boisei*	*Early Homo*	

referred to as *H. ergaster*) occurred during the same time period in northern Kenya. *Homo erectus* (*ergaster*), early genus *Homo*, and *Australopithecus robustus* all occurred in South Africa between 1.6 and 1.9 million years ago (Wood 1992). *Australopithecus aethiopicus* and *Australopithecus garhi* lived within a few hundred kilometers of each other in East Africa 2.5 million years ago (Walker et al. 1986; Asfaw et al. 1999). And in southern Africa, fossilized remains of *Australopithecus robustus* and *Homo habilis* have been found in the same fossil deposits (Broom 1950; Grine et al. 1993). It appears that *Australopithecus afarensis* also had a close relative, *Kenyanthropus platyops*, that lived in the same region of east Africa at about 3.5 million years ago (Johanson & White 1979; Leakey et al. 2001). Fossil dating is not always precise, and a more complete fossil record may someday yield evidence of three or even four species coexisting in some of these areas. If early hominids were like all other high animals, such coexistence implies a history of competition between the species. The nature of that competition would have been a key influence on which lineages eventually survived, which ones went extinct, and which one evolved into *Homo sapiens*.

Our ability to understand such patterns of sympatry is severely limited, however, by the lack of modern analogs to extrapolate from, eventhough sympatric relations in other sympatric primates have been studied for decades. For example, Pierre Charles-Dominique (1977) studied the coexistence of five sympatric prosimians (lorises and galagos) in a West African forest in the 1970s. He found that although all were roughly the same body size and general phenotype, each species had either a dietary specialty (beetle larvae vs. fruits) or a unique pattern of foraging (forest canopy vs. understory) that effectively lessened potential competition among them. Robert Sussman (1974) found the same effect between two Madagascar lemurs (*Eulemur fulvus* and *Lemur catta*). John Terborgh (1983) found much the same niche-division pattern among several species of New World monkeys in an Amazon rain forest in Peru. Anne Gautier-Hion and Jeanne-Paul Gautier (1983) also found a similar pattern for Old World monkeys in an African forest.

Unfortunately, however, there are few opportunities for this sort of research with direct implications for human evolution, because there are no other living hominids except ourselves. This is where chimpanzees and gorillas come in, giving us a window onto the behavior and ecology of two closely related, anatomically similar hominoids sharing the same habitat.

COEXISTENCE AND DIET

There are some basic dietary differences that were apparent in this study, which in general agree with the few previous findings about sympatric great apes. The Kyagurilo gorillas rely on terrestrial herbaceous vegetation, or THV, the salad of leafy greens that covers the ground at Bwindi, as a lean season staple or fallback food (Nkurunungi 2005). Gorillas elsewhere do the same (Doran & McNeilage 1998). Chimpanzees do not, although one study (Wrangham et al. 1991) found that chimpanzees feeding on THV was inversely correlated with fruit-eating, suggesting THV might be a fallback food among chimpanzees at times, too. We found no evidence of this in Bwindi chimpanzees, though our analyses of chimpanzee diet were limited by the lack of identification of herbaceous plant material. We have no nutritional information on the most important plant species. There has been a debate over whether gorillas seek fatty fruits (Calvert 1985) or avoid them (Rogers et al. 1988), and whether chimpanzees use figs as a preferred fruit source (Janzen 1979) or a fallback food (Wrangham et al. 1993). The debate over the value of figs rests on the relative nutritional versus harvesting-efficiency benefits of a diet that includes large quantities of figs. We cannot resolve these issues with the current data set, but it is clearly an important aspect of the ecological difference between gorillas and chimpanzees.

Watts (1991) and Yamagiwa et al. (1996) found that where gorilla groups and chimpanzee communities share the same forest, the two species exploit resources differently. Gorilla groups tend to "harvest" small sections of their home range each month, covering the entire home range only over the course of an entire year. Chimpanzees forage far and wide on a daily basis, covering a large percentage of their home range in a shorter time period. When their preferred fruits are scarce, the community disperses into small subgroups, larger foraging parties forming mainly when ripe fruit is abundant (Goodall 1986). These very different foraging strategies may also allow chimps and gorillas to exist in the same forest while avoiding feeding competition. Another important factor in Bwindi may be that despite the gorillas' greater reliance on fruit relative to mountain gorillas in the Virungas, Bwindi gorillas' mean daily travel distance is only about 100 meters farther than that of the Virunga gorillas (Nkurunungi 2005). Elsewhere, gorilla daily path length is positively correlated with the amount of fruit consumed (Remis 1997; Goldsmith 1999; Stanford 2006a), which suggests that other factors, such as Bwindi's extremely rugged terrain and the necessity of frequent steep uphill climbs, may also affect travel distance.

The idea that chimpanzees and gorillas all across Africa may be ecologically separated based on chimpanzees' greater reliance on fruit is supported by a comparison of the effect of increasing elevation on the level of fruit consumption for each species in study sites of varying elevations. Among gorilla populations, there is a statistically significant negative relationship between elevation and frugivory (see Chapter 5). Gorillas living at high elevations in the Virungas eat almost no fruit, whereas lowland populations eat a diet rich in fruit. But there is no such relationship between elevation and frugivory among chimpanzee populations, which eat mainly fruit everywhere and tend not to live in forests that are not fruit-rich.

CHIMPANZEE–GORILLA DIETARY DIFFERENCES

One interesting dietary finding in the study was that although we never observed hunting or meat-eating by the Ruhija chimpanzees, and red colobus—the main prey of chimps elsewhere—do not occur in Bwindi, the Ruhija chimpanzees nevertheless ate meat. We found evidence of meat-eating in the fecal samples comparable to what has been reported from other chimpanzee study sites. We could not tell whether prey had been killed or scavenged when already dead, but there was clear evidence of consumption of monkeys (probably *Cercopithecus l'hoesti*, a common semi-terrestrial species; Stanford & Nkurunungi 2003) and duiker antelope.

The great apes vary widely in their willingness to include the meat of other mammals in their diets. Of the four great apes, only chimpanzees hunt and eat mammalian prey systematically enough to truly be consider omnivores (Goodall 1986; Stanford 1998). Although their overall meat consumption is minor compared to nearly all human societies (Kaplan et al. 2000; Finch & Stanford 2004), chimpanzees are highly efficient and avid predators. In some studies, chimpanzee communities have consumed more than 1,000 kilogram of meat annually, and as much as 0.5 kilogram per week per individual (Stanford et al. 1994a; Stanford 1998). On the other hand, bonobos capture monkeys but don't seem to regard them as food items (SabaterPi et al. 1993) and gorillas show little interest in eating vertebrates at all.

Everywhere chimpanzees have been studied, from rain forest to savanna, they have been observed to hunt. Males and females both hunt, but most kills (91% at Gombe, Tanzania, since 1982; Stanford et al. 1994b) are by adult and adolescent males hunting in groups. Hunting is a normal component of chimpanzee behavioral ecology, not pathological or human-influenced behavior. Hunting data on minimally human-influenced chimpanzees in the Taï National Park have, for instance, shown a pattern similar to both Mahale and Gombe (Boesch & Boesch 1989).

Chimpanzees are omnivores, in that a small portion of their diet is composed of meat; the bulk of their diet is ripe fruit, foliage, and invertebrates. Gombe chimpanzee diet includes about 3% meat (Teleki 1973; Goodall 1986; McGrew 1992). The small percentage of meat in the diet does not mean the amount of meat consumed is trivial. In 1990 and 1992, the estimated biomass of colobus monkeys eaten by the Kasakela community at Gombe was 452 kilograms and 517 kilograms, respectively (Stanford 1998). The portion of the chimpanzee diet that is meat is therefore quite large and approaches the figures for the low end of the range of human hunter-gatherer people. For example, the Efe foragers of the Ituri forest, Zaïre, get 8.5% of their calories from meat (Bailey & Peacock 1988).

Chimpanzees and gorillas in Bwindi are confronted with the same available resources, which includes access to animal fat, protein, and calories in the form of mammalian prey (and also scavengeable carcasses).

Chimpanzees in Bwindi eat meat, but gorillas do not. The explanation for this difference could be ecological, behavioral, energetic, or physiological. We tend to assume that gorillas are too big and bulky to hunt other animals as chimpanzees do. But field research (Tutin et al. 1996; Kuroda 1996) has shown clearly that gorillas climb tall trees. Chimpanzee predatory behavior is done mainly by males and its success relies on group action (Stanford et al. 1994b). Gorillas may not hunt because most groups contain only one adult male, and when two or more silverbacks occur together, they do not engage in communal behaviors that contribute to hunting success. There are, however, some anecdotal accounts of gorillas failing to show interest in prey even when it presents itself. Schaller (1963, p. 167) observed adult gorillas in the Virungas ignoring duiker carcasses, bush pig carcasses, and nesting doves, all of which were within easy capture. Gorillas simply are not interested in eating meat.

Gorillas may not eat meat in the wild because of a long history of natural selection for full-fledged herbivory. Chimpanzees not only eat meat eagerly, but also are well designed to digest it (Milton & Demment 1989). There is some evidence that the ability to eat a diet high in saturated fats without suffering the health consequences may have been a key physiological adaptation that occurred as the hominid lineage diverged from the ancestral lineage of chimpanzees and gorillas (Finch & Stanford 2004). Nelson et al. (1984) reported that captive gorillas fed a commercial diet with the same saturated fat content as chimpanzees had significantly higher cholesterol levels. Zoo gorillas are maintained on diets severely restricted in saturated fats because of the risk of heart disease, particularly in adult males (Meehan, personal communication). Gorillas may restrict their consumption of animal fats of all sorts; they consume insects, but not nearly as systematically as chimpanzees do.

THE EVOLUTION OF CHIMPANZEE AND GORILLA DIETS

In the Miocene period of Earth's history, between approximately 22 and 6 million years ago, the early evolution and diversification involved a wide variety of ape species, some of which coexisted (Hill & Ward 1988). By the early Pliocene just afterward, a radiation of early hominids began. A number of bipedal, small-brained hominids evolved and occupied both forested and open habitats in eastern (Johanson & White 1979; Asfaw et al. 1999) and central (Brunet et al. 2002) Africa. The full extent of this diversification of hominids is still unknown, but recent discoveries (Asfaw et al. 1999; Leakey et al. 2001) suggest that bipedalism may not have been a unique hallmark of the hominid lineage. Instead, bipedalism likely evolved in more than one lineage, with at least two continuing into the Pliocene. We know, for instance, of at least two separate but contemporaneous bipedal lineages, *Australopithecus* and *Kenyanthropus*, at 3.5 million years ago.

During early eras of human evolution, the hominid diet indisputably expanded to include the meat of other mammals. If some ancestral ape lineages included meat in the diet, those species might have gained a competition-avoidance edge in coping with the presence of other related forms in the same habitat. In other words, if one ancestral ape was an omnivore and another in the same habitat was not, a key aspect of niche separation would have been achieved. We can speculate that mutations occurred in human evolution that increased the hominid tolerance to dietary fat (Cordain et al. 2001, 2002; Finch & Stanford 2004). Hillard Kaplan and colleagues (2000) have extended this idea to the evolution of intelligence and longevity. If even modest omnivory was a key dietary shift enabled by the evolution of tolerance to cholesterol and fat, it would help to explain how multiple early hominoid species, including the earliest hominids, could have lived sympatrically while avoiding direct feeding competition.

If omnivory was one aspect of the divergence between the ancestral ape niches, it would help explain the striking contrast in meat-eating between chimpanzees and gorillas. Bonobos, which shared a common ancestor with chimpanzees as recently as one million years ago (Gagneux et al. 1996), do not consume meat as often or as eagerly as chimpanzees do. Some researchers (Hohmann & Fruth 1993) believe that bonobo meat-eating has been underestimated in the wild. I have argued that the female-dominant nature of bonobo society make males less interested in hunting for meat themselves (Stanford 1998).

Including meat in the diet appears to be one underappreciated aspect of the ecological separation of sympatric chimpanzees and gorillas. If true, it could also be strongly inferred as a point of distinction among sympatric ancestral apes. As early hominids evolved in Africa during the late Miocene and early Pliocene, one of the many ways in which competition was avoided was through the development of diverse diets. Some of these species likely turned to omnivory as a way to avoid competition.

WHAT WOULD ANCIENT HOMINID COEXISTENCE HAVE BEEN LIKE?

Certainly sympatric Miocene apes or Pliocene hominids did not share resources in the same way that living great apes do. Each case is unique and using any one species as a model is bound to be simplistic. However, we can infer some likely aspects of sympatric ecology.

Diet

Sympatric early hominids must have had diets that differed in key ways. This is predicted by ecological theory and supported by the observed differences in tooth pattern between gracile and robust hominids that were sympatric in East Africa during the Pliocene. The dichotomies might have been subtle, and perhaps only came into play during lean times. Robust australopithecines, with their oversized molar teeth, might have used their dental adaptations to open hard-shelled or fibrous plant foods only during times of drought or food scarcity, or only in some habitats in which small-molared gracile hominids also occurred. The data on African ape sympatry from my study and others is that robust and gracile australopithecines may have had very similar diets, differing only subtly or seasonally, but enough to allow coexistence.

Competition

Direct head-to-head, or contest, feeding competition would occur if sympatric fossil apes or early hominids ate the same species of fruit. One species would probably be dominant to its sympatric counterpart, forcing the subordinate species to become a more efficient forager (Houle 2004). Limited evidence from the Bwindi study suggests that a smaller-bodied ape (chimpanzees) is ecologically dominant to a larger-bodied one (gorillas). Ecological dominance would, however, not be visible in the fossil record.

Omnivory

An omnivorous species might coexist with a frugivorous or folivorous one. The number of prey and amount of meat could be small but still be a point of niche separation. Skeletal anatomy does not provide reliable cues about meat-eating; gorillas have large canines and available prey but don't eat meat. Likewise, skeletal adaptations for arboreality and traits that might be associated with predatory behavior are not necessarily related to omnivory.

Travel Patterns

Sympatric species with divergent diets will also have different foraging patterns and daily travel patterns. Fruit-eaters will range further than leaf-eaters and fruit specialists (like chimpanzees) will travel farther than opportunistic fruit-eaters like gorillas.

Nesting Patterns

Chimpanzees occasionally nest on the ground in Bwindi and at a few other sites. In Bwindi, ground nesting is found only where gorillas do not live. This may be due to a long history of nest site competition. It could also, however, be an indirect effect of different diets, in that one species may nest in proximity to plant food species on which it feeds.

Grouping Patterns

Mating systems can influence ranging patterns; there is much evidence that large groups travel farther each day than small groups (Janson & Goldsmith 1995). Sympatric large-bodied hominoids might have had to cope with limited food resources, with natural selection causing two species to diverge in their grouping patterns, which in turn would mold their diets in different directions.

You must bear in mind that the four living great apes are a small remnant of a much larger and more diverse lineage millions of years ago. Both anatomy and behavior were diverse, and sympatric fossil ape ecology might have resembled those of modern associations of multiple monkey species in the same forests. Hominid species diversity in the Pliocene did not approach that of apes in the Miocene. Future studies, both of great apes and of human and ape fossils, will no doubt shed much more light on the questions raised in this book. It is almost certain that future research will uncover more cases of likely sympatry among early hominids as well as early apes. As long as we infer cautiously and conservatively, the great apes still have a great deal to teach us about our own family origins.

Epilogue

I formally ended the BIGAPE project in December 2005. It would have been easy to continue sending funds there, and making periodic trips to check on its progress. The primary reason I ended the sympatric chimpanzee–gorilla study was that, having decided not to attempt to more fully habituate the Ruhija chimpanzees to our presence, we had reached a point of diminishing returns in terms of research data. The decision not to habituate more was a pragmatic one; the terrain and undergrowth made it extremely difficult to follow the animals, even after years spent watching them from a safe distance through binoculars. In addition, we had always worried that if the chimpanzees became very tame and then our project ended, they could be approached easily and killed by poachers, having lost their fear of people.

There were other reasons to stop as well. Bwindi, despite the beefed-up security following the 1999 attacks, had never felt to me a safe enough place to bring my children. Having my family living in a nearby town, hours from the research project, never seemed like a good alternative either, so I had made all my field trips alone for nearly a decade, and this had begun to wear on me. I had also become involved in another primate research project in China, on the rare golden snub-nosed monkey (*Rhinopithecus roxellana*) in 2002 (Li et al. 2002), and wanted to devote myself to that project more fully. After fifteen years working in East Africa, I was also eager to return to Asia, where I had conducted my graduate thesis research many years earlier, to begin new projects. Some researchers thrive and contribute by staying in the same research site year after year, often for their entire careers. I have always had a need to move on to new projects, new species, and new ideas after a few years.

Today, much research continues at Bwindi. Bosco is working with ITFC and some of the foreign gorilla researchers there. Gervase has returned to his family in Nkuringo Valley, but also works for ITFC on ecological projects. Evarist caught on, this time as a field assistant rather than a camp keeper, with Michele Goldsmith's tourism research project for a time. The ITFC itself is thriving; with a new hilltop telecommunications system in place in the Ruhija research station, researchers spend their day hiking after the mountain gorillas and come home to read today's *New York Times* online. The team of field assistants continues to track the Kyagurilo gorillas. A Ugandan Ph.D. student, Fortunate Myambi, is doing some ecological research on the Ruhija chimpanzees; after that their future as a known study population is uncertain. Alastair McNeilage continues to steer research at Bwindi in the right directions and manage the station in Ruhija. Martha Robbins, Jessica Rothman, and other expatriate researchers continue to come and go, contributing to the overall effort to fully understand the lives of Bwindi apes.

In Buhoma, ecotourism is bustling once again, with international tour companies ferrying in wealthy tourists. At last report (late 2005), the cost per person of visiting the tourist gorilla groups had risen to nearly $400 per hour. Even at this price, the luxury tented camps and lodges are operating at nearly full capacity. Buhoma, and its gorillas, may become victims of their own success, however. Every year more buildings are erected, and Buhoma has grown from a cozy and quiet ecologically sensitive camp to a veritable town. At the current rate of development, there will be a negative impact on the gorillas in years to come, either from encroachment on the forest habitat, or from refuse dumping or some similar health risk brought on by human population density. Although there are laws and policies that are intended to control ecotourism development, these are often set aside when well-funded tour companies come seeking government approval for projects.

In Nkuringo, tourism has begun in earnest. UWA has built a tourist camp, some of it on land sold to UWA by Gervase and Evarist (who had made shrewd land speculations using their BIGAPE salaries during the years when tourism in Nkuringo was anticipated). The former BIGAPE camp near Nkuringo, abandoned after the 1999 rebel attack, has never been reoccupied. Although I haven't visited the site in years, Gervase tells me it is hard to tell there was ever a camp there. With time, the land will hopefully regrow its forest and become part of the buffer zone on the park's perimeter, shielding the gorillas and chimpanzees from direct contact with humans to some extent.

The Nkuringo gorillas now see people more than ever, as a result of the start of full-scale ecotourism there. Nothing more is known about the Nkuringo chimpanzees than we knew at the time of the attacks. Although some gorilla research is being carried out in Nkuringo, it is mainly concerned with health issues for the gorillas that arise from close human contact. My guess is that researchers will return to Nkuringo at some point to learn more about the forest and its inhabitants, although with the Congo border walking distance away, the security situation in that part of Bwindi will never be ideal.

As for the animals themselves, the Kyagurilo gorillas continue to thrive in Ruhija, but with some notable changes. After years of life on the periphery of the group, Rukina, now a full-fledged silverback, began to challenge Zeuss. Instead of retreating in the face of Zeuss's threats, Rukina stood his ground, and increasingly launched attacks of his own. After six months of such intense aggression, Rukina succeeded; Zeuss died in December 2004 of injuries inflicted during fights with Rukina. The younger male, now in his twenties, is the lone silverback in the Kyagurilo group. The group today consists of fourteen animals, thanks to several recent births. Females Binyindo, Siatu, Matu, Tindamanyire, and Mugwere are still in the group, along with four subadult males (Marembo, Sikio, Byiza, and Fuzi), two juveniles (Bizibu and Mukiza), and three infants (Kabandize, Thursday, and Happy).

The Ruhija chimpanzees and gorillas will continue, I hope, to lead quiet lives full of the same joys that our own lives are made of: good relationships with their kin and allies, courtship, birth and watching members of their group grow up, and limited stress from disease and other causes of mortality. They richly deserve it.

Appendix

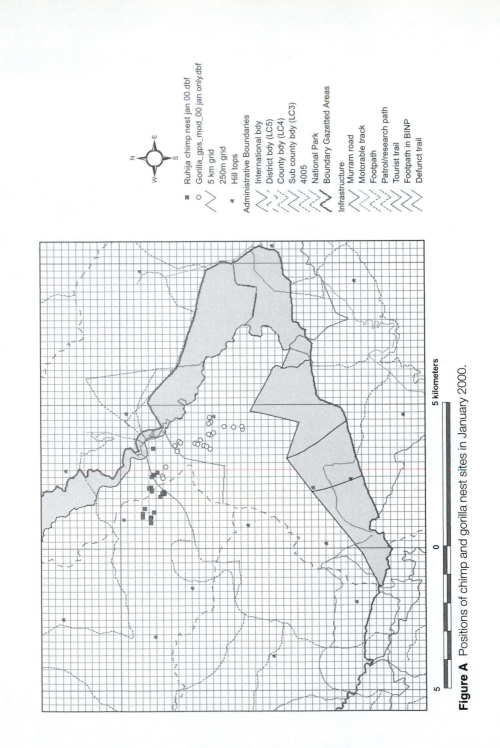

Figure A Positions of chimp and gorilla nest sites in January 2000.

Ruhija chimp nest jan 00.dbf
Gorilla_gps_mod_00 jan only.dbf
5 km grid
250m grid
Hill tops
Administrative Boundaries
International bdy
District bdy (LC5)
County bdy (LC4)
Sub county bdy (LC3)
4005
National Park
Boundary Gazetted Areas
Infrastructure
Murram road
Motorable track
Footpath
Patrol/research path
Tourist trail
Footpath in BINP
Defunct trail

5 kilometers

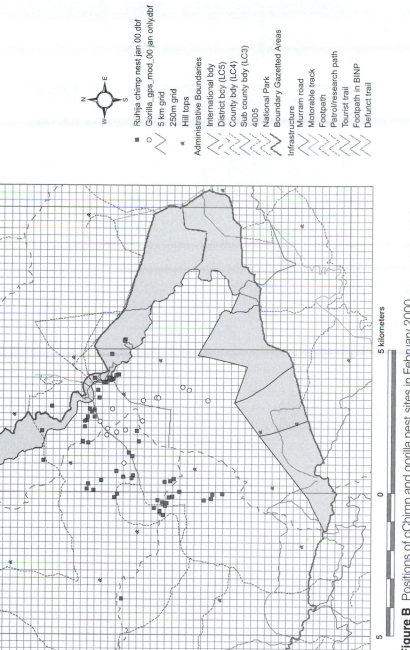

Ruhija chimp nest jan 00.dbf
Gorilla_gps_mod_00 jan only.dbf
5 km grid
250m grid
Hill tops

Administrative Boundaries
International bdy
District bcy (LC5)
County bdy (LC4)
Sub county bdy (LC3)
4005
National Park
Boundary Gazetted Areas

Infrastructure
Murram road
Motorable track
Footpath
Patrol/research path
Tourist trail
Footpath in BINP
Defunct trail

5   0   5 kilometers

Figure B Positions of cChimp and gorilla nest sites in February 2000.

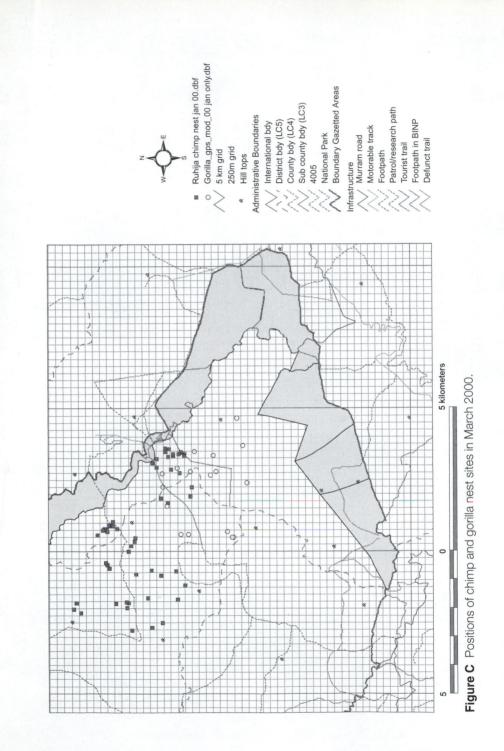

Figure C Positions of chimp and gorilla nest sites in March 2000.

Ruhija chimp nest jan 00.dbf
Gorilla_gps_mod_00 jan only.dbf
5 km grid
250m grid
Hill tops
Administrative Boundaries
International bdy
District bdy (LC5)
County bdy (LC4)
Sub county bdy (LC3)
4005
National Park
Boundary Gazetted Areas
Infrastructure
Murram road
Motorable track
Footpath
Patrol/research path
Tourist trail
Footpath in BINP
Defunct trail

5 kilometers

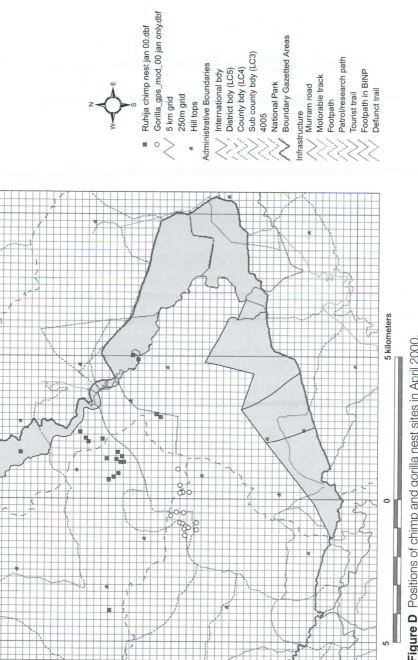

Figure D Positions of chimp and gorilla nest sites in April 2000.

Ruhija chimp nest jan 00.dbf
Gorilla_gps_mod_00 jan only.dbf
5 km grid
250m grid
Hill tops
Administrative Boundaries
International bdy
District bdy (LC5)
County bdy (LC4)
Sub county bdy (LC3)
4005
National Park
Boundary Gazetted Areas
Infrastructure
Murram road
Motorable track
Footpath
Patrol/research path
Tourist trail
Footpath in BINP
Defunct trail

5   0   5 kilometers

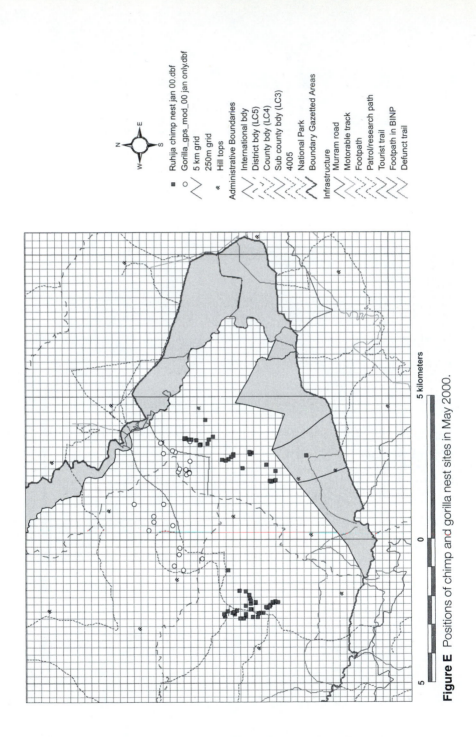

Figure E Positions of chimp and gorilla nest sites in May 2000.

Ruhija chimp nest jan 00.dbf
Gorilla_gps_mod_00 jan only.dbf
5 km grid
250m grid
Hill tops

Administrative Boundaries
International bdy
District bdy (LC5)
County bdy (LC4)
Sub county bdy (LC3)
4005
National Park
Boundary Gazetted Areas

Infrastructure
Murram road
Motorable track
Footpath
Patrol/research path
Tourist trail
Footpath in BINP
Defunct trail

N
W   E
S

5   0   5 kilometers

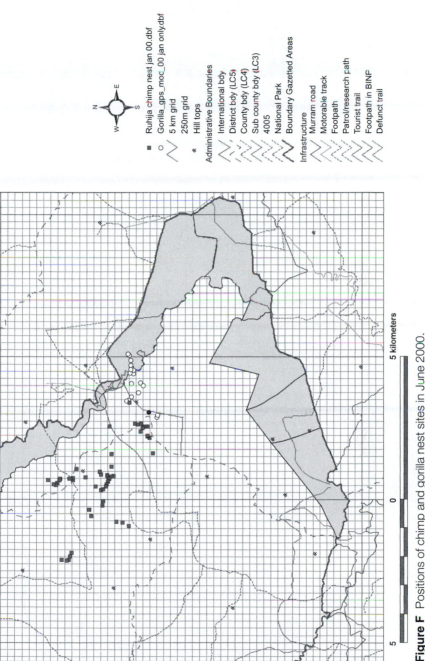

N
W E
S

■ Ruhija chimp nest jan 00.dbf
○ Gorilla_gps_moc_00 jan only.dbf
5 km grid
250m grid
✳ Hill tops

Administrative Boundaries
International bdy
District bdy (LC5)
County bdy (LC4)
Sub county bdy (LC3)
4005
National Park
Boundary Gazetted Areas

Infrastructure
Murram road
Motorable track
Footpath
Patrol/research path
Tourist trail
Footpath in BINF
Defunct trail

5   0   5 kilometers

Figure F Positions of chimp and gorilla nest sites in June 2000.

117

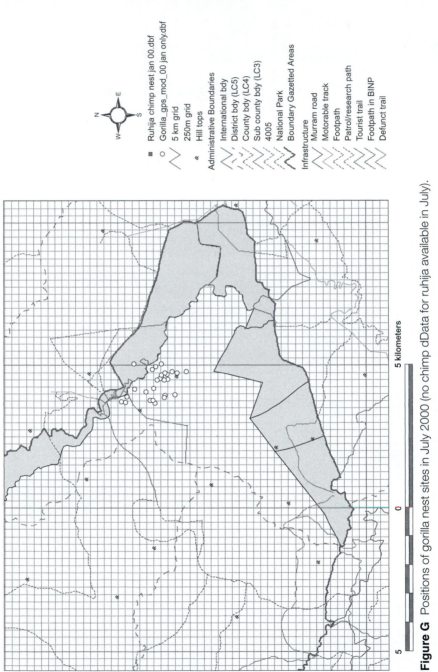

Figure G Positions of gorilla nest sites in July 2000 (no chimp dData for ruhija available in July).

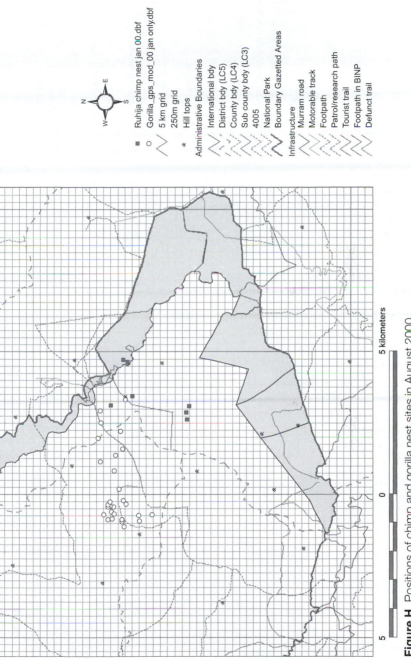

Figure H Positions of chimp and gorilla nest sites in August 2000.

Ruhija chimp nest jan 00.dbf
Gorilla_gps_mod_00 jan only.dbf
5 km grid
250m grid
Hill tops
Administrative Boundaries
International bdy
District bdy (LC5)
County bdy (LC4)
Sub county bdy (LC3)
4005
National Park
Boundary Gazetted Areas
Infrastructure
Murram road
Motorable track
Footpath
Patrol/research path
Tourist trail
Footpath in BINP
Defunct trail

5 kilometers

5   0   5

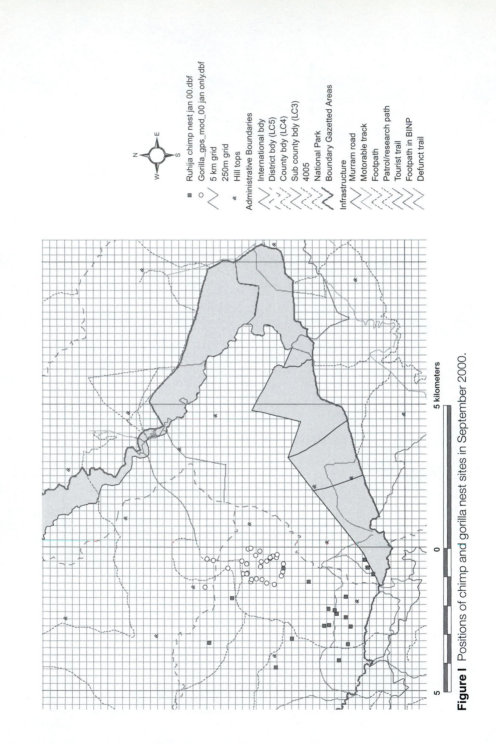

Figure I Positions of chimp and gorilla nest sites in September 2000.

Ruhija chimp nest jan 00.dbf
Gorilla_gps_mod_00 jan only.dbf
5 km grid
250m grid
Hill tops
Administrative Boundaries
International bdy
District bdy (LC5)
County bdy (LC4)
Sub county bdy (LC3)
4005
National Park
Boundary Gazetted Areas
Infrastructure
Murram road
Motorable track
Footpath
Patrol/research path
Tourist trail
Footpath in BINP
Defunct trail

5 kilometers

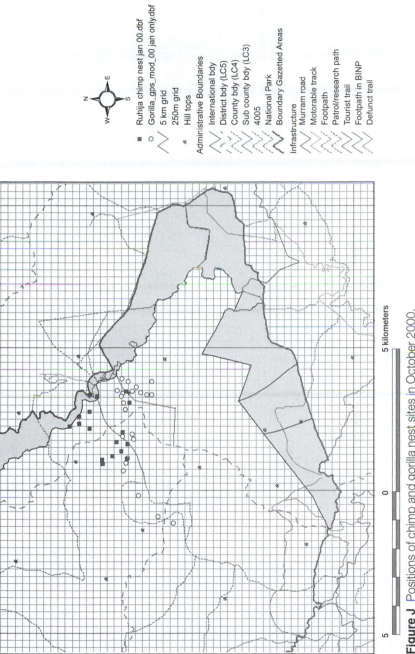

Figure J Positions of chimp and gorilla nest sites in October 2000.

Ruhija chimp nest jan 00.dbf
○ Gorilla_gps_mod_00 jan only.dbf
5 km grid
250m grid
Hill tops
Administrative Boundaries
International bdy
District bdy (LC5)
County bdy (LC4)
Sub county bdy (LC3)
4005
National Park
Boundary Gazetted Areas
Infrastructure
Murram road
Motorable track
Footpath
Patrol/research path
Tourist trail
Footpath in BINP
Defunct trail

5 kilometers

5   0   5

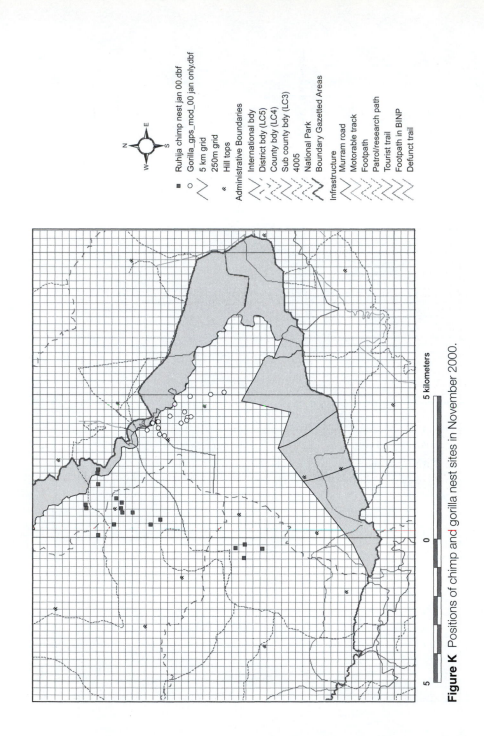

Figure K Positions of chimp and gorilla nest sites in November 2000.

Ruhija chimp nest jan 00.dbf
Gorilla_gps_mod_00 jan only.dbf
5 km grid
250m grid
Hill tops
Administrative Boundaries
International bdy
District bdy (LC5)
County bdy (LC4)
Sub county bdy (LC3)
4005
National Park
Boundary Gazetted Areas
Infrastructure
Murram road
Motorable track
Footpath
Patrol/research path
Tourist trail
Footpath in BINP
Defunct trail

5 kilometers

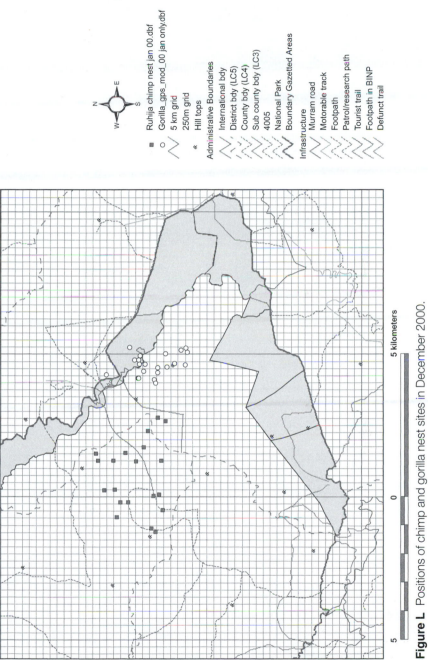

Figure L Positions of chimp and gorilla nest sites in December 2000.

Ruhija chimp nest jan 00.dbf
Gorilla_gps_mod_00 jan only.dbf
5 km grid
250m grid
Hill tops
Administrative Boundaries
International bdy
District bdy (LC5)
County bdy (LC4)
Sub county bdy (LC3)
4005
National Park
Boundary Gazetted Areas
Infrastructure
Murram road
Motorable track
Footpath
Patrol/research path
Tourist trail
Footpath in BINP
Defunct trail

5 kilometers

5   0   5

References

Asfaw, B., T. White, and G. Suwa. 1999. *Australopithecus garhi:* A New Species of Early Hominid from Ethiopia. *Science* 284: 629–635.

Bailey, R. C., and N. R. Peacock. 1988. Efe Pygmies of Northeast Zaïre: Subsistence Strategies in the Ituri Forest. In *Coping with Uncertainty in Food Supply,* eds., I. de Garine and G. A. Harrison, 88–117. Oxford: Clarendon Press.

Baldwin, P. J., J. Sabater Pi, W. C. McGrew, and C. E. G. Tutin. 1981. Comparison of Nests Made by Different Populations of Chimpanzees (*Pan troglodytes*). *Primates* 22: 474–486.

Basabose, K., and J. Yamagiwa. 1997. Predation on Mammals by Chimpanzees in the Montane Forest of Kahuzi, Zaïre. *Primates* 38: 45–55.

Bauer, H. R. 1977. Chimpanzee Bipedal Locomotion in the Gombe National Park, East Africa. *Primates* 18: 913–921.

Boesch, C., and H. Boesch. 1989. Hunting Behavior of Wild Chimpanzees in the Taï National Park. *American Journal of Physical Anthropology* 78: 547–573.

Boesch, C., and H. Boesch. 1990. Tool Use and Tool Making in Wild Chimpanzees. *Folia Primatologica* 54: 86–99.

Bradley B. J., Robbins M. M., Williamson E. A., Steklis H. D., Steklis N. G., Eckhardt N., Boesch C., and Vigilant L. 2005. Mountain Gorilla Tug-of-War: Silverbacks Have Limited Control over Reproduction in Multimale Groups. *Proceedings National Academy of Sciences* 102 (26): 9418–9423.

Broom, R. 1950. The Genera and Species of the South African Fossil Ape-men. *American Journal of Physical Anthropology* 8: 1–1.

Brunet, M., Guy, F., Pilbeam, D., Mackaye, H. T., Likius, A., Ahounta, D., Beauvilain, A., Blondel, C., Bocherens, H., Boisserie, J. R., De Bonis, L., Coppens, Y., Dejax, J., Denys, C., Duringer, P., Eisenmann, V., Fanone, G., Fronty, P., Geraads, D., Lehmann, T., Lihoreau, F., Louchart, A., Mahamat, A., Merceron, G., Mouchelin, G., Otero, O., Campomanes, P. P., De Leon, M. P., Rage, J. C., Sapanet, M., Schuster, M., Sudre, J., Tassy, P., Valentin, X., Vignaud, P., Viriot, L., Zazzo, A., and Zollikofer, C. 2002. A New Hominid from the Upper Miocene of Chad, Central Africa. *Nature* 418: 145–151.

Calvert, J. J. 1985. Food Selection by Western Lowland Gorillas *(G.g. gorilla)* in Relation to Food Chemistry. *Oecologia* 65: 236–246.

Casimir, M. J., and E. Butenandt. 1973. Migration and Core Area Shifting in Relation to Some Ecological Factors in a Mountain Gorilla Group (*Gorilla g. beringei*) in Mt. Kahuzi region (Republique du Zaïre). *Zeitschrift Tierpsychologie* 33: 514–522.

Chapman, C. A., F. J. White, and R. Wrangham. 1994. Party Size in Chimpanzees and Bonobos: A Reevaluation of Theory Based on Two Similarly Forested Sites. In *Chimpanzee Cultures*, eds. Wrangham R. W., McGrew W. C., de Waal F. B. M., and Heltne P. G., 41–57. Cambridge, MA: Harvard University Press.

Charles-Dominique, P. 1977. *Ecology and Behavior of Nocturnal Primates*. New York: Columbia University Press.

Cody, M., and J. Diamond, eds. 1975. *Ecology and Evolution of Communities*. Cambridge, MA: Harvard University Press.

Cordain, L., J. B. Miller, S. B. Eaton, N. Mann, S. H. A. Holt, and J. D. Speth. 2001. Plant–Animal Subsistence Rations and Macronutrient Energy Estimations in Worldwide Hunter-Gatherer Diets. *American Journal of Clinical Nutrition* 71: 682–692.

Cordain, L., S. B. Eaton, J. B. Miller, N. Mann, N., and H. Kaplan. 2002. The Paradoxical Nature of Hunter-Gatherer Diets: Meat-based, yet Nonatherogenic. *European Journal of Clinical Nutrition* 56 (Supplement): 1–11.

Crawley, M. J., ed. 1986. *Plant Ecology*. Oxford: Blackwell Scientific Publications.

Delgado, R. A., and C. P. van Schaik. (2000). The Behavioral Ecology and Conservation of the Orangutan (*Pongo pygmaeus*): A Tale of Two Islands. *Evolutionary Anthropology* 9: 201–218.

de Waal, F. B. M., and F. Lanting. 1997. *Bonobo: The Forgotten Ape*. Berkeley: University of California Press.

Djojosudharmo, S., and C. P. van Schaik. 1992. Why Are Orangutans so Rare in the Highlands? Altitudinal Changes in a Sumatran Forest. *Tropical Biodiversity* 1: 11–22.

Doran, D. M. 1993. Sex Differences in Adult Chimpanzee Positional Behavior: The Influence of Body Size on Locomotion and Posture. *American Journal of Physical Anthropology* 91: 99–115.

Doran, D. M., and A. McNeilage. 1998. Gorilla Ecology and Behavior. *Evolutionary Anthropology* 6: 120–131.

Falk, D. 1990. Brain Evolution in *Homo:* The "Radiator" Theory. *Behavior and Brain Science* 13: 333–381.

Finch, C. E., and C. B. Stanford. 2004. Meat-adaptive Genes and the Evolution of Slow Aging Rates in Humans. *Quarterly Review Biology* 79: 1–50.

Fossey, D., and A. H. Harcourt. 1977. Feeding Ecology of Free-ranging Mountain Gorillas (*Gorilla gorilla beringei*). In ed., T. H. Clutton-Brock, *Primate Ecology* 415–447. New York: Academic Press.

Fruth, B., and G. Hohmann. 1993. Ecological and Behavioural Aspects of Nest Building in Wild Bonobos (*Pan paniscus*). *Ethology* 94: 113–126.

Fruth, B., and G. Hohmann. 1996. Nest Building in the Great Apes: The Great Leap Forward? In *Great Ape Societies,* ed. W. C. McGrew, L. Marchant, and T. Nishida, 225–240. New York: Cambridge University Press.

Furuichi, T. 1989. Social Interactions and the Life History of Female Pan paniscus in Wamba, Zaïre. *International Journal of Primatology* 10: 173–198.

Furuichi, T., C. Hashimoto, and Y. Tashiro. 2001. Fruit Availability and Habitat Use by Chimpanzees in the Kalinzu Forest, Uganda: Examination of fallback foods. *International J Primatol* 22: 929–946.

Gagneux, P., C. Wills, U. Gerloff, D. Tautz, Morin, P. A., Boesch, C., Fruth, B., Hohmann, G., Ryder, O. A., and Woodruff, D. S. 1996. Mitochondrial Sequences Show Diverse Evolutionary Histories of African Hominoids. *Proceedings of National Academy of Sciences,* 5077–5082.

Galdikas, B. 1985. Orangutan Sociality at Tanjing Putting. *American Journal of Primatology* 9: 101–119.

Garner, K. J., and O. A. Ryder. 1996. Mitochondrial DNA Diversity in Gorillas. *Molecular Phylogenetics and Evolution* 6: 39–48.

Gautier-Hion, A., Quris, A. R., and J. P. Gautier. 1983. Monospecific vs. Polyspecific Life: A Comparative Study of Foraging and Antipredatory Tactics in a Community of *Cercopithecus* Monkeys. *Behavioral Ecology and Sociobiology* 12: 325–335.

Gebo, D. L. 1996. Climbing, Brachiation, and Terrestrial Quadrupedalism: Historical Precursors of Hominid Bipedalism. *American Journal of Physical Anthropology* 101: 55–92.

Ghiglieri, M. P. 1984. *The Chimpanzees of the Kibale Forest.* New York: Columbia University Press.

Goldberg, T., and R. Wrangham. 1997. Genetic Correlates of Social Behaviour in Wild Chimpanzees: Evidence from Mitochondrial DNA. *Animal Behaviour* 54: 559–570.

Goldsmith, M. L. 1999. Ranging Behavior of a Lowland Gorilla (*Gorilla g. gorilla*) Group at Bai Hokou, Central African Republic. *International Journal of Primatology* 20: 1–23.

Goodall, A. G. 1977. Feeding and Ranging in the Kahuzi Gorillas. In *Primate Ecology,* ed. T. H. Clutton-Brock 450–478. London: Academic Press.

Goodall, J. 1968. Behaviour of Free-Living chimpanzees of the Gombe Stream Area. *Animal Behaviour Monographs* 1: 163–311.

Goodall, J. 1986. *The Chimpanzees of Gombe: Patterns of Behavior.* Cambridge: Harvard University Press.

Grine, F. E., B. Demes, W. L. Jungers, and T. M. Cole III. 1993. Taxonomic Affinity of the Early Homo Cranium from Swartkrans, South Africa. *American Journal of Physical Anthropology* 92: 411–426.

Hamilton, A. C., D. Taylor, and J. C. Vogel. 1986. Early Forest Clearance and Environmental Degradation in South-west Uganda. *Nature* 320: 164–167.

Hasegawa, Y., and M. Hiraiwa-Hasegawa. 1983. Opportunistic and Restrictive Matings among Wild Chimpanzees in the Mahale Mountains, Tanzania. *Journal of Ethology* 1: 75–85.

Hernandez, A. 2006. Behavioral Ecology of Arid Country Chimpanzees at Issa River, Tanzania. Ph.D. dissertation, University of Southern California.

Herre, E. A., C. A. Machado, E. Bermingham, J. D. Nason, D. M. Windsor, S. S. McCafferty, W. V. Houten, and K. Bachmann. 1996. Molecular Phylogenies of Figs and their Pollinator Wasps. *Journal of Biogeography* 23: 521–530.

Hohmann, G., and B. Fruth. 1993. Field Observations on Meat Sharing among Bonobos (*Pan paniscus*). *Folia Primatologica* 60: 225–229.

Houle, A. 2004. Mechanisms of Coexistence among the Frugivorous Primates of Kibale National Park, Uganda. Ph.D. dissertation, Université du Quebec á Montréal.

Houle, A., W. L. Vickery, and C. A. Chapman. In press. Mechanisms of Coexistence among Two Species of Frugivorous Primates. *Journal of Animal Ecology*.

Hunt, K. D. 1994. The Evolution of Human Bipedality: Ecology and Functional Morphology. *Journal of Human Evolution* 26: 183–202.

Hunt, K. D. 1996. The Postural Feeding Hypothesis: An Ecological Model for the Evolution of Bipedalism. *South African Journal of Science* 92: 77–90.

Hunt, K. D. 1998. Ecological Morphology of *Australopithecus afarensis*. In *Primate Locomotion*, ed. E. Strasser, 397–418. New York: Plenum Press.

Jablonski, N. G., and G. Chaplin. 1993. Origin of Habitual Terrestrial Bipedalism in the Ancestor of the Hominidae. *Journal of Human Evolution* 24: 259–280.

Janzen, D. H. 1979. How to Be a fig. *Annual Review Ecology and Systematics* 10: 13–51.

Johanson, D. C., and T. D. White. 1979. A Systematic Assessment of Early African Hominids. *Science* 202: 321–330.

Johanson, D. C., C. O. Lovejoy, W. H. Kimbel, T. D. White, S. C. Ward, M. E. Bush, B. M. Latimer, and Y. Coppens. 1982. Morphology of the Pliocene Partial Hominid skeleton (AL 288-1) from the Hadar Formation, Ethiopia. *American Journal of Physical Anthropology* 57: 403–452.

Jolly, C. J. 1970. The Seed-eaters: A New Model of Hominid Differentiation Based on a Baboon Analogy. *Man* 5: 1–26.

Jones, C., and J. Sabater Pi. 1971. Comparative Ecology of *Gorilla gorilla* (Savage and Wyman) and *Pan troglodytes* (Blumembach) in Rio Muni, West Africa. *Bibliotheca Primatologica* 13: 1–95.

Jungers, W. L. 1982. Lucy's Limbs: Skeletal Allometry and Locomotion in *Australopithecus afarensis*. *Nature* 297: 676–678.

Kano, T. 1992. *The Last Ape*. Stanford, CA: Stanford University Press.

Kaplan, H., K. Hill, J., Lancaster, and A. M. Hurtado. 2000. A Theory of Human Life History Evolution: Diet, Intelligence, and Longevity. *Evolutionary Anthropology* 9: 156–185.

Keith, A. 1923. Man's Posture: Its Evolution and Disorders. *British Medical Journal* 1: 451–454, 499–502, 545–548, 587–590, 624–626, 669–672.

Knott, C. D. 1998. Changes in Orangutan Caloric Intake, Energy Balance, and Ketones in Response to Fluctuating Fruit Availability. *International Journal of Primatology* 19: 1061–1079.

Kuroda, S. 1992. Ecological Interspecies Relationships between Gorillas and Chimpanzees in the Ndoki-Nouabale Reserve, Northern Congo. In *Topics in Primatology, Volume 2: Behavior, Ecology, and Conservation,* eds. N. Itoigawa, Y. Sugiyama, G. P. Sackett, and R. K. R. Thompson, 385–394. Tokyo: Tokyo University Press.

Kuroda, S., T. Nishihara, S. Suzuki, and R. Oko. 1996. Sympatric chimpanzees and gorillas in the Ndoki Forest, Congo. In *Great Ape Societies* eds. W. C. McGrew, L. F. Marchant, and T. Nishida, 71–81. Cambridge: Cambridge University Press.

Leakey, L. S. B. 1959. A New Fossil Skull from Olduvai. *Nature* 184: 491–493.

Leakey, L. S. B. 1966. *Homo habilis, Homo erectus,* and the Australopithecines. *Nature* 209: 1279–1281.

Leakey, M. G., Spoor, F., Brown, F. H., Gathogo, P. N., Kiarie, C., Leakey, L. N., and McDougall, I. 2001. New Hominin Genus from Eastern Africa Shows Diverse Middle Pliocene Lineages. *Nature* 410: 433–440.

Leighton, M. 1993. Modeling Diet Selectivity by Bornean Orangutans: Evidence for Integration of Multiple Criteria for Fruit Selection. *International Journal of Primatology* 14: 257–313.

Leonard, W. R., and Robertson, M. L. 1997. Rethinking the Energetics of Bipedality. *Current Anthropology* 38: 304–309.

Lovejoy, C. O. 1981. The Origin of Man. *Science* 211: 341–350

Lovejoy, C. O. 1988. The Evolution of Human Walking. *Scientific American* 259: 118–125.

Maggioncalda, A. N., Czekala, N. M., and Sapolsky, R. M. 2002. Male Orangutan Subadulthood: A New Twist on the Relationship between Chronic Stress and Developmental Arrest. *American Journal of Physical Anthropology* 118: 25–32.

Matsumoto-Oda, A. Hosaka, K., Huffman, M. A., and Kawanaka, K. 1998. Factors Affecting Party Size in Chimpanzees of the Mahale Mountains. *International Journal of Primatology* 19: 1013–1028.

McGrew, W. C. 1992. *Chimpanzee Material Culture.* Cambridge: Cambridge University Press.

Milton, K., and M. Demment. 1989. Features of Meat Digestion by Captive Chimpanzees (*Pan troglodytes*). *American Journal of Primatology* 18: 45–52.

Mitani, J. C., D. A. Merriwether, and C. Zhang. 2000. Male Affiliation, Cooperation and Kinship in Wild Chimpanzees. *Animal Behaviour* 59: 885–893.

Mitani, J. C., D. Watts, and J. Lwanga. 2002. Ecological and Social Correlates of Chimpanzee Party Size and Composition. In *Behavioral Diversity in Chimpanzees and Bonobos,* eds. C. Boesch, G. Hohmann, and L. F. Marchant, 248–258. Cambridge: Cambridge University Press.

Morgan, D., and C. Sanz. In press. Chimpanzee Feeding Ecology and Comparisons with Sympatric Gorillas in the Goualougo Triangle, Republic of Congo. In *Primate Feeding Ecology in Apes and Other Primates,* eds. G. Hohmann, M. Robbins, and C. Boesch. New York: Cambridge University Press.

Muller, M., E. Mpongo, C. B. Stanford, and C. Boehm. 1995. A Note on the Scavenging Behavior of Wild Chimpanzees. *Folia Primatologica* 65: 43–47.

Muller, M. N., and R. W. Wrangham. 2004. Dominance, Cortisol and Stress in Wild Chimpanzees (*Pan troglodytes schweinfurthii*). *Behavioral Ecology and Sociobiology* 55: 332–340.

Nelson, C. A., Greer, W. E., and Morris, M. D. 1984. The Distribution of Serum High Density Lipoprotein Subfractions in Nonhuman Primates. *Lipids* 19: 656–663.

Newton-Fisher, N., Reynolds, V., and Plumptre, A. 2001. Food Supply and Chimpanzee Party Size in the Budongo Forest Reserve, Uganda. *International Journal of Primatology* 21: 613–628.

Nishida, T. 1979. The Social Structure of Chimpanzees of the Mahale Mountains. In *The Great Apes*, eds. D. A. Hamburg, and E. R. McCown 73–122. London: Benjamin/Cummings.

Nishida, T. 1990. A Quarter Century of Research in the Mahale Mountains: An Overview. In *The Chimpanzees of the Mahale Mountains*, ed. T. Nishida, 3–36. Tokyo: University of Tokyo Press.

Nishihara, T. 1995. Feeding Ecology of Western Lowland Gorilla in the Nouabale-Ndoki National Park, Congo. *Primates* 36: 151–168.

Nkurunungi, J. B. 2005. The Availability and Distribution of Fruit and Non-fruit Plant Resources in Bwindi: Their Influence on Gorilla Habitat Use and Food Choice. Ph.D. dissertation, Makerere University.

Nkurunungi, J. B., T. White, and C. B. Stanford. In press. GIS Analysis of Range Use by Sympatric Mountain Gorillas and Chimpanzees in Bwindi Impenetrable National Park, Uganda. In *Primates of Western Uganda*, eds. J. Paterson, V. Reynolds, and H. Notman, Kluwer-Plenum. New York, pp. 193–205.

Nkurunungi, J. B., J. Ganas, M. Robbins, and C. B. Stanford. 2004. A Comparison of Two Mountain Gorilla Habitats in Bwindi Impenetrable National Park, Uganda. *African Journal of Ecology* 42: 289–297.

Parish, A. R. 1996. Female Relationships in Bonobos (*Pan paniscus*). *Human Nature* 7: 61–96.

Pickford, M., and Senut, B. 2001. "Millennium Ancestor," a 6-million-Year-Old Bipedal Hominid from Kenya—Recent Discoveries Push Back Human Origins by 1.5 Million Years. *South African Journal of Science* 97: 2–22.

Plumptre, A.J., and V. Reynolds. 1997. Nesting Behavior of Chimpanzees: Implications for Censuses. *International Journal of Primatology* 18: 475–485.

Prost, J. H. 1980. Origins of Bipedalism. *American Journal of Physical Anthropology* 52: 175–190.

Quiatt, D., Reynolds, V., and Stokes, E. J. 2002. Snare Injuries to Chimpanzees (*Pan troglodytes*) at 10 Study Sites in East and West Africa. *African Journal of Ecology* 40: 303–305.

Remis, M. J. 1997. Ranging and Grouping Patterns of a Western Lowland Gorilla Group at Bai Houkou, Central African Republic. *American Journal of Primatology* 43: 111–133.

Rijksen, H. 1978. *A Field Study on Sumatran Orangutans*. Wageningen: H. Veenman and Zonen.

Rodman, P. S. 1977. Feeding Behavior of Orangutans in the Kutai Reserve, East Kalimantan. In *Primate Ecology,* ed. T. H. Clutton-Brock, 383–413. London: Academic Press.

Rodman, P. S., and H. M. McHenry. 1980. Bioenergetics and the Origin of Hominid Bipedalism. *American Journal of Physical Anthropology* 52: 103–106.

Rogers, M. E., E. A. Williamson, C. E. G. Tutin, and M. Fernandez. 1988. Effects of the Dry Season on Gorilla Diet in Gabon. Primate Report: *Selected Proceedings of the XIIth IPS-Congress* 22: 25–33.

Rose, M. D. 1984. Food Acquisition and the Evolution of Positional Behavior: The Case of Bipedalism. In *Food Acquisition and Processing in Primates,* ed. D. J. Chivers, B. A. Wood, and A. Bilsborough, 509–524, New York: Plenum Press.

Sabater Pi, J., M. Bermejo, G. Ilera, and J. J. Vea. 1993. Behavior of Bonobos (*Pan paniscus*) Following their Capture of Monkeys in Zaïre. *International Journal Primatology* 14: 797–804.

Sarmiento, E., T. Butynski, and J. Kalina. 1996. Ecological, Morphological, and Behavioral Aspects of Gorillas of Bwindi-Impenetrable and Virungas National Parks, with Implications for Gorilla Taxonomic Affinities. *American Journal of Primatology* 40: 1–21.

Schaller, G. B. 1963. *The Mountain Gorilla.* Chicago: University of Chicago Press.

Sept, J. 1998. Shadows on a Changing Landscape: Comparing Nesting Patterns of Hominids and Chimpanzees since Their Last Common Ancestor. *American Journal of Primatology* 46: 85–101.

Sicotte, P. 2001. Female Mate Choice in Mountain Gorillas. In *Mountain Gorillas,* eds. M. Robbins, P. Sicotte, and K. J. Stewart, 59–88. Cambridge: Cambridge University Press.

Stanford, C. B. 1995. The Influence of Chimpanzee Predation on Group Size and Anti-predator Behaviour in Red Colobus Monkeys. *Animal Behaviour* 49: 577–587.

Stanford, C. B. 1998. *Chimpanzee and Red Colobus: The Ecology of Predator and Prey.* Cambridge, MA: Harvard University Press.

Stanford, C. B. 2001. The Subspecies Concept in Primatology: The Case of Mountain Gorillas. *Primates* 42: 309–318.

Stanford, C. B. 2002. Arboreal Bipedalism in Bwindi Chimpanzees. *American Journal of Physical Anthropology* 119: 87–91.

Stanford, C. B. 2006a. The Sympatric Ecology of African Great Apes: with Implications for the Hominoid divergeace. *Primates* 47: 91–101.

Stanford, C. B. 2006b. Arboreal Bipedalism in Wild Chimpanzees: Implications for Models of the Evolution of Hominid Posture and Locomotion. *American Journal of Physical Anthropology.* 129: 225–231.

Stanford, C. B., and J. B. Nkurunungi. 2003. Sympatric Ecology of Chimpanzees and Gorillas in Bwindi Impenetrable National Park, Uganda. Diet. *International Journal of Primatology* 24: 901–918.

Stanford, C. B., J. Wallis, H. Matama, and J. Goodall. 1994a. Patterns of Predation by Chimpanzees on Red Colobus Monkeys in Gombe National Park, Tanzania, 1982–1991. *American Journal of Physical Anthropology* 94: 213–228.

Stanford, C. B., J. Wallis, E. Mpongo, and J. Goodall. 1994b. Hunting Decisions in Wild Chimpanzees. *Behaviour* 131: 1–20.

Stern, J. T., and Susman, R. L. 1983. The Locomotor Anatomy of *Australopithecus afarensis*. *American Journal of Physical Anthropology* 60: 279–317.

Steudel, K. L. 1994. Locomotor Energetics and Hominid Evolution. *Evolutionary Anthropology* 3: 42–48.

Strong, D. R. Jr., D. Simberloff, L. G. Abele, and A. B. Thistle, eds. 1984. *Ecological Communities: Conceptual Issues and the Evidence*. Princeton, NJ: Princeton University Press.

Susman, R. L. ed. 1984. *The Pygmy Chimpanzee*. New York: Plenum Press.

Sussman, R. W. 1974. Ecological Distinctions in Sympatric Species of Lemur. In *Prosimian Biology* eds. R. D. Martin, G. A. Doyle, and A. C. Walker, 75–108. London: Duckworth.

Takahata, Y., Hasegawa, T., and Nishida, T. 1984. Chimpanzee Predation in the Mahale Mountains from August 1979 to May 1982. *International Journal of Primatology* 5: 213–233.

Teleki, G. 1973. *The Predatory Behavior of Wild Chimpanzees*. Lewisburg, PA: Bucknell University Press.

Terborgh, J. 1983. *Five New World Primates*. Princeton, NJ: Princeton University Press.

Tutin, C. E. G. 1996. Ranging and Social Structure of Lowland Gorillas in the Lopé Reserve, Gabon. In *Great Ape Societies*, eds. W. C. McGrew, L. F. Marchant, and T. Nishida, 58–70. Cambridge: Cambridge University Press.

Tutin, C. E. G., and M. Fernandez. 1985. Foods Consumed by Sympatric Populations of *Gorilla g. beringei* and *Pan t. troglodytes* in Gabon: Some Preliminary Data. *International Journal of Primatology* 6: 27–43.

Tutin, C. E. G., and M. Fernandez. 1993. Composition of the Diet of Chimpanzees and Comparisons with that of Sympatric Lowland Gorillas in the Lopé Reserve, Gabon. *American Journal of Primatology* 30: 195–211.

Tutin, C. E. G., W. C. McGrew, and P. Baldwin. 1983. Social Organization of Savanna-dwelling Chimpanzees, *Pan troglodytes verus*, at Mt. Assirik, Senegal. *Primates* 24: 154–173.

Tuttle, R. H. 1981. Evolution of Hominid Bipedalism and Prehensile Capabilities. *Philosophical Transactions of Royal Society of London, Series B (Biological Sciences)* 292: 89–94.

Van Schaik, C. P., Azwar, and D. Priatna. 1995. Population Estimates and Habitat Preferences of Orangutans based on Line Transects of Nests. In *The Neglected Ape*, eds. R. D. Nadler, B. M. F. Galdikas, L. K. Sheeran, and N. Rosen, 129–147. New York: Plenum Press.

Vedder, A. L. 1984. Movement Patterns of a Group of Free-ranging Mountain Gorillas (*Gorilla gorilla beringei*) and Their Relation to Food Availability. *American Journal of Primatology* 7: 73–88.

Videan E., and W. C. McGrew. 2001. Are Bonobos (*Pan paniscus*) really More Bipedal than Chimpanzees (*Pan troglodytes*)? *American Journal of Primatology* 54: 233–239.

Washburn, S. L. 1968. Speculation on the Problem of Man's Coming to the Ground. In *Changing Perspectives on Man*, ed. B. Rothblatt, 191–206. Chicago: University of Chicago Press.

Walker, A., R. L. Leakey, J. M. Harris, and E. H. Brown. 1986. 2.5 Myr *Australopithecus boisei* from West of Lake Turkana, Kenya. *Nature* 322: 517–522.

Waller, J. C., and Reynolds, V. 2001. Limb Injuries Resulting from Snares and Traps in Chimpanzees (*Pan troglodytes schweinfurthii*) of the Budongo Forest, Uganda. *Primates* 42: 135–139.

Watts, D. P. 1984. Composition and Variability of Mountain Gorilla Diets in the Central Virungas. *American Journal of Primatology* 7: 323–356.

Watts, D. P. 1989. Infanticide in Mountain Gorillas: New Cases and a Reconsideration of the Evidence. *Ethology* 81: 1–18.

Watts, D. P. 1991. Strategies of Habitat Use by Mountain Gorillas. *Folia Primatologica* 56: 1–16.

Watts, D. P. 1998. Long-Term Habitat Use by Mountain Gorillas. 2. Reuse of Foraging Areas in Relation to Resource Abundance, Quality, and Depletion. *International Journal of Primatology* 19: 681–702.

Watts, D. P. 2001. Social Relationships of Female Mountain Gorillas. In *Mountain Gorillas*, eds. M. Robbins, P. Sicotte, and K. J. Stewart, 215–240. Cambridge: Cambridge University Press.

Wheeler, P. E. 1984. The Evolution of Bipedality and Loss of Functional Body Hair in Hominids. *Journal of Human Evolution* 13: 91–98.

Whiten, A., J. Goodall, W. C. McGrew, T. Nishida, V. Reynolds, Y. Sugiyama, C. E. G. Tutin, R. W. Wrangham, and C. Boesch. 1999. Cultures in Chimpanzees. *Nature* 399: 682–685.

Williamson, E. A., C. E. G. Tutin, M. E. Rogers, and M. Fernandez. 1990. Composition of the Diet of Lowland Gorillas in Gabon. *American Journal of Primatology* 21: 265–277.

Wilson, M. L., M. D. Hauser, and R. W. Wrangham. 2001. Does Participation in Intergroup Conflict Depend on Numerical Assessment, Range Location, or Rank for Wild Chimpanzees? *Animal Behaviour* 61:1203–1216.

Wood, B. A. 1992. Origin and Evolution of the genus *Homo*. *Nature* 355: 783–790.

Wrangham, R. W. 1975. Behavioural ecology of chimpanzees in Gombe National Park, Tanzania. Ph.D. dissertation, Cambridge University.

Wrangham, R. W., N. L. Conklin, C. A. Chapman, and K. D. Hunt. 1991. The Significance of Fibrous Foods for Kibale Forest Chimpanzees. *Philosophical Transactions of the Royal Society of London (Series B)* 334: 171–178.

Wrangham, R. W. 1999a. Why Are Male Chimpanzees more Gregarious than Mothers? A Scramble Competition Hypothesis. In *Male Primates*, ed. P. Kappeler 248–258. Cambridge: Cambridge University Press.

Wrangham, R. W. 1999b. The Evolution of Coalitionary Killing. *Yearbook of Physical Anthropology* 42: 1–30.

Wrangham, R. W., N. L. Conklin, G. Etot, K. D. Hunt, M. D. Hauser, and A. P. Clark. 1993. The Value of Figs to Chimpanzees. *International Journal of Primatology* 14: 243–256.

Yamagiwa, J. 2001. Dispersal Patterns, Group Structure, and Reproductive Parameters of Eastern Lowland Gorillas at Kahuzi in the Absence of Infanticide. In *Mountain Gorillas,* eds. M. Robbins, P. Sicotte, and K. J. Stewart, 89–122. Cambridge: Cambridge University Press.

Yamagiwa, J., N. Mwanza, T. Yumoto, and T. Maruhashi. 1994. Seasonal Change in the Composition of the Diet of Eastern Lowland Gorillas. *Primates* 35: 1–14.

Yamagiwa, J., T. Maruhashi, T. Yumoto, and N. Mwanza. 1996. Dietary and Ranging Overlap in Sympatric Gorillas and Chimpanzees in Kahuzi-Biega National Park, Zaïre. In *Great Ape Societies,* eds. W. C. McGrew, L. F. Marchant, and T. Nishida, 82–98. Cambridge: Cambridge University Press.

Index